# how Human can you get?

## Charles Martin

InterVarsity Press
Downers Grove
Illinois 60515

© 1973 by
Inter-Varsity Press, London

First American printing
October 1973
by InterVarsity Press
with permission from
Inter-Varsity Fellowship,
London.

InterVarsity Press
is the book publishing
division of Inter-Varsity
Christian Fellowship.

ISBN 0-87784-359-7
Library of Congress Catalog
Card Number: 73-81576

Printed in the United
States of America

# Contents

# Introduction:

# Human predicament or human enterprise?

'Perhaps they have the first opportunity in history to *invent the human being*', says Kathleen Nott in her contribution to *The Humanist Outlook*. A startling phrase for a bold idea. The 'they' are Humanists. She is not all that pleased with their progress to date, but feels they have this great opportunity 'to establish Humanism as what it has been in glimpses and moments – an examination of the real possibilities of the real concrete human being'.[1]

This is one of the more optimistic current statements about humanity. We are surrounded by plenty of pessimistic ones. On all sides we are invited to wallow in the human predicament, its suffering, its insensibility, the spectres of over-population, famine, illiteracy, and final extermination if pollution or war are not brought under control. Yet two-thirds of the British public lose little sleep over such matters. Life is there, and they get on and live it in a more or less cheerful, rule-of-thumb, day-to-day manner. Their newspapers do not carry ponderous discussions of the human enterprise nor drag them through the human predicament, but simply present them with 'human interest' and the sports pages. They watch some serious TV programmes but these often give them a superficial feeling of knowing 'what is going on in the world' and after ten or twenty minutes' 'discussion' between experts most issues are apparently buttoned up.[2]

[1] A. J. Ayer (ed.), *The Humanist Outlook* (Pemberton, 1968), p. 180.
[2] It could be argued in fact that by far the more serious communica-

High falutin' economic theory leaves them cold, but the down-to-earth facts about the pay packet and the price-tags in the supermarket are understood all too well. They resolutely tell Gallup-pollsters that they believe in God but don't go to church, except for weddings, funerals – and more rarely, nowadays, for baptisms. In many ways broadly tolerant, and aiming for 'the good life', they are 'the majority' for whom genuine, signed-up members of the British Humanist Association claim to speak, and the 'outsiders' whom Christians try unsuccessfully to lure into their churches.

The other third – though a third may be a generous fraction – are God's gift to publishers. With either self-conscious duty or genuine enjoyment they wade through the ponderous magazines and learned editorials; they devour highbrow paperbacks and haunt the non-fiction shelves of the local libraries. They write to each other through the correspondence columns of the same magazines and newspapers; they talk endlessly about life, the good life, the common life, how it should be organized and lived – until the cynic may say they have no time or energy to live it. Of this third a large proportion is the student population who awake with fresh vigour in the late evening and talk half-way through the night; who read paperbacks as others read shopping lists, and who are extraordinarily well-informed on at least one side of every question. You name it, they've thought about it, read about it, possibly even written about it. Within this bookish group come the majority of Christians and the overwhelming majority of pledged Humanists.[3] Both claim inarticulate support from the 'two-thirds', inter-preting and counter-interpreting opinion poll statistics to

tion of values and ideals goes on through 'Crossroads', 'Coronation Street' and some of the lyrics broadcast in 'Top of the Pops'.

[3] Of 931 members of the British Humanist Association questioned in 1964, 59% had university degrees or professional qualifications, 97% were in the Registrar General's scale I, II and III, the other 3% being 'partly skilled' and none of 'unskilled occupation' (*Sociological Review*, November 1965).

show that the man in the street is really with them though he doesn't express it very well. Both make the occasional foray among the unlettered to get their support, or vote, or to try to bring them the good news or to improve their social lot.

Perhaps things have been like this for a long time, except that 100 years ago the proportions of 'others' to 'bookish' were nearer nine-tenths and one-tenth. What is new in the more recent situation is the change in relative affluence, mobility and authority patterns. The publishers may not get much out of the two-thirds, but the travel agents do; so do the local garage and do-it-yourself store. And this freedom from economic and local limitation has loosened the attitudes to authority and standards. The bookish no longer have automatic authority and status. The pay packet has no strings. The worker does what he likes in his own time – though it will usually be decent, neighbour-regarding stuff, the harmless devotion at the new shrines of car and garden. The ten or twenty minutes' 'discussion' on the TV show him, anyway, that there are at least as many of the bookish in favour of his free-and-easy life-style as there are calling him to sterner paths of duty and respect for the establishment.

Now where, in all this, is the 'opportunity to invent the human being'? Where, for that matter, is the opportunity for men and women to grow, as the apostle Paul put it, 'to mature manhood, measured by nothing less than the full stature of Christ'[4] – an option not restricted to the twentieth century? Clearly a great deal of our answer will depend upon what we think it is to be 'a human being', and it is to this question that the present book is directed. It does not set out to give an ordered doctrine of man from Christian, Humanist or other viewpoints; excellent primers of this nature are already available.[5]

[4] Ephesians 4: 13.
[5] *E.g.* T. M. Kitwood, *What is Human?* (IVP, 1970); H. J. Blackham, *Humanism* (Penguin, 1968).

Nor is it intended to be the 'plain Christian's guide to what is wrong with Humanism', though it is written from a Christian viewpoint and will have to say from time to time where Humanists appear to have cut the human possibility short. It is written at the more modest level of discovering what it is to be human, in the hope that Christians and Humanists – usually among the bookish – may take time off from digging their entrenched positions deeper and look about them. Christians may find that humanity contains more than they imagined and that some of their barricades have been in the wrong places. Humanists may gain confidence to peer into the cupboard that holds the skeleton of abandoned childhood Christianity. Both may be given humility to consider the multitude who do not read their books or pamphlets but who may, in fact, turn out to be human after all.

Why pick on Christians and Humanists? Because broadly they cover the two main ways of looking at life. Either man is on his own and must get on with it as best he can, or he has company in the universe and his wisdom will lie in finding out what sort of company it is. There are other alternatives. Communism will be briefly looked at, and there are things we can learn from non-Christian religions. But the narrow area selected contains quite enough muddle and misconception to sort out at one go.

'What is man?' said the psalmist 3,000 years ago, and the question is now back in the centre of discussion once more. But the intervening 3,000 years have seen a lot of discovery and a lot of confusion. Twentieth-century natural and social sciences are highly developed systems of thought; philosophers have littered the world with theory and counter-theory; the small agricultural community of the psalmist has given way to the jungle of the city and the extraordinary complexity of commerce and industry. Modern man is bewildered and confused.

Among the bookish, part of the confusion is caused by

failure to realize how language is used. The phenomenal success of the scientific method has bemused them into thinking that science has the 'real' explanations, that scientific descriptions are the most accurate and reliable. But human experience is not exhausted by these descriptions. Hence the method of the present book will be to deal with three commonly-used systems of language: molecule-talk, the language of science; me-talk, the language of personal experience; us-talk and them-talk, the language of inter-personal relationships. These areas of language are all useful in dealing with experience. Everyone uses them all, frequently, but often jumps from one to the other without realizing it. Worse still, people sometimes talk as if statements in different language systems are contradictory. The systems are, in fact, autonomous – in the sense that no statement in one system can be attacked or confirmed by a statement in another. For example, my sensation of 'choosing' what to do is not in conflict with the psychological account of stimulus and response mechanisms. *Both* statements can be true, each in its own system. More will be said about this as the discussion proceeds – together with a look at 'God-talk', a fourth frame of language that Christians claim is essential to the full expression of human experience.

# 1 Molecules makyth man

Perhaps it would be truer to say that man makes molecules, or thinks them up anyway. The explosion of scientific knowledge is a very real factor in the present situation. It is the reason behind Kathleen Nott's hope that *now*, at this late stage in human history, we have an outstanding opportunity to invent the human being. The long apprenticeship to slow biological evolution is over; the secrets of life are out; man can take over his own development; psycho-social evolution begins. So Julian Huxley argued in his impressive introduction to *The Humanist Frame*[1] and it is a noble picture. In previous ages men lived by hunch, superstition or the twilight of limited experience. Now we know how things work – or at least are well on the way to knowing. Nature is an open book. The keys of knowledge are in the scientist's hands, and are rapidly bringing him the power to control his environment and direct his future. In a couple of hundred breath-taking years man has come out from under the weight of circumstance and has taken charge of his own affairs.

## Science – slave or tyrant?
Or has he? Not everyone, even in the Humanist camp, is so sanguine about man's control over nature. Man's control over nature turns out, as C. S. Lewis reminded

[1] Julian Huxley (ed.), *The Humanist Frame* (Allen and Unwin, 1961), pp. 13ff.

us, to be one man's control over another. What disturbs us is not the power but who wields it. Can men be trusted with such control? Will it exercise a dread fascination so that what *can* be done, must be done, whether it is a trip to Mars or a brain transplant? Every new technological achievement is met with cries of admiration and alarm, often from the same people. Norman Moss gives an example in his book *Men who play God*, the story of the hydrogen bomb. Writing of the American physicist Edward Teller he says:

'He lives still in that spirit that has dominated Western civilization since the late eighteenth century, equating human good with education, reason and the spread of knowledge into dark places, the spirit that has underlaid and motivated scientific progress.

Some lost the optimism that stemmed from this attitude and these values on the Somme or in Flanders . . . . others when they saw the rise in crime and violence that accompanied increasing education and prosperity.

The atomic scientists lost it with Hiroshima and Nagasaki.

Teller never lost his optimistic faith in the values of the Enlightenment. No doubts or scruples slowed his resolve to build the hydrogen bomb. He is the physicist before the Fall, who has not known sin. For Teller, widespread protests about radiation are the voice of superstition. . . . He looks on the test-ban advocates as a biological experimenter looks on the anti-vivisectionists.

Teller had no thought of drawing back from arrogating power over man and nature for fear of playing God, since new knowledge of nature, power over environment, the power to change worlds, can be knowledge and power for good in the right hands. As an optimist, he has no doubts that the right hands exist.'[2]

Pollution has taken over from the bomb as the chief point of anxiety and chief centre for protest, but the problems are the same. Can men be trusted with their power to manipulate their planet home? Humanists are well aware of the dangers but feel we must press on – with something of the exhilaration of riding a dangerous horse at full gallop. Christians have less cause than most to trust man's good will, and show a wide range of re-actions. A small minority weave dire forebodings out of isolated texts. Some see fresh evidence of the Creator's design and power. Some would like to retreat to the (imagined) more comfortable days before plastics and nuclear fission were thought of. Behind much of these is another, deeper, dread.

## Science – friend or foe?

Will this explosion of scientific knowledge help the Christian cause? Does it not lead to just that pride in man which is the root of all sin? The rise of scientific achieve-ment has correlated closely with the decline of English churchmanship. Humanists rush to say the God of miracles is no longer required; science has displaced him. Many Christians, afraid that this might well happen, have accordingly fought the advancing stream of scien-tific knowledge, trying to find at least some dry land where God could reign inviolate. A considerable body of recent writing suggests that in this enterprise they have been mistaken.[3] Rather should they see the advance of scientific knowledge as banishing the nature gods and spirits of paganism. In Newbigin's words, 'man is in-vited, if he will, to become God's son and heir and to

[2] N. Moss, *Men who play God* (Penguin, 1970), p. 88.
[3] *E.g.* M. A. Jeeves, *The Scientific Enterprise and Christian Faith* (Tyndale Press, 1969); C. Davis, *God's Grace in History* (Fontana, 1966); J. Habgood, *Religion and Science* (Mills and Boon, 1964).

have freedom of the whole estate subject only to his obedience to the Father'. As to the Humanist's boasting of mastery, Newbigin warns us, 'The possibility that men might be masters of the created world is not contemplated; the two possibilities are slavery and sonship.'[4]

The sad fact is, however, that Humanists have a firm picture of Christians as obscurantist, afraid of science, struggling against all evidence to save the irrational and the supernatural. Hence their confidence in science is increased the more, till a modern Habakkuk might echo the taunt against the Chaldeans, 'he sacrifices to his net and burns incense to his seine; for by them he lives in luxury, and his food is rich'. Net and seine may have given way to the atomic pile and the laser beam as the tools which man now uses, but the pathetic confidence is the same. To this we shall return from time to time, but for the moment let us try to find out what molecules have made of man.

## The chemical description of man

To the chemist man is a complex collection of chemicals; quite ordinary elements whose properties are well known – well-behaved molecules combining regularly and predictably. Some of the combinations are highly complex and fascinating but gradually the story has been told of amino-acids, proteins, enzymes and even the marvellous double helix of DNA. In 1953 Crick and Watson announced their discoveries of these intricate molecules that transmit genetic characteristics. The blue eyes, fair hair and perhaps even the talent for mathematics could all be traced to the nucleic acids on the DNA strands. The miracles of blood, muscle and nerve are all reduced to ordered patterns of biochemical laws. Man is a collection of common chemicals – mostly carbon, with a dash of phosphorus, enough iron to make a six-inch nail and enough sulphur to rid one dog of

[4] L. Newbigin, *Honest Religion for Secular Man* (SCM, 1966), p. 32.

fleas – together with about a hundredweight of water. Say 50p the lot.

To put this together in the right order is, of course, another matter. It costs a small fortune in fact to synthesize any one of the dozens of amino-acids the body makes all day. Christians ought to rejoice at this demonstration of the Genesis story – '*out of the ground* the Lord God formed man'; the same stuff is in both. Also, oddly enough, science has reinstated *real* matter – the idealistic arguments about everything being in the mind seem long ago. Science deals with stuff that is *there*, though molecules, atoms, electrons, seem to get less and less 'solid'. Science can't say where matter or energy originally came from and doesn't ask. Humanists tend to say it's no good asking that sort of question, anyway. Matter is here; get on and find out how it works. Christians have their revelation of creation – God giving being to matter, matter that can be investigated rationally, with reliable laws, because he is a reliable, rational God.

Both Christian and Humanist often feel a sense of wonder at the complexity of nature, the beauty and order of the structures they discover, the economy and ingenuity of the human body. Christian apologists argue that this is strong evidence for a Designer. Humanists take refuge in 'chance mutations' or 'trends' in billions of years of evolution. But Christians have often not stopped to wonder and worship at the chemist's discoveries. Instead they have rushed on to ask the wrong question: If it's all just molecules, where's the soul? Unbelievers have helped on the discomfiture, asking how survival of personality fares when the dust returns to the earth as it was. Anthony Flew, for example, in a book review, commends 'this assault on behalf of the view which sees man as essentially corporeal, and against the view which holds that the real me is somehow essentially incorporeal. And this is a difference which for many reasons matters enormously: because it is only if the second view is correct that it could even begin to be plausible to suggest that we shall survive death.'[5] More recently, Professor F. A. E. Crew in a moving essay on the meaning of death declares, 'I am persuaded that when once life is launched it must reach its final destination which is death and that death implies the extinction of the individual and the dissolution of the worldstuff of which he is composed into its primordial elements which return to the universe, dust to dust and ashes to ashes.'[6]

So where's the pie in the sky when you die? Everything's all labelled up with chemical tags waiting to rot down in the nitrogen cycle or go up the crematorium chimney.

But the Humanist crows and the Christian cringes too early. The sword is too sharp and cuts off more than the assailant wishes. For 'What happens when you disintegrate?' only leads to 'What's happening when the bits are working?' Where am 'I' in this whirl of molecules? The relation of 'mind' to 'brain' is not to be lightly answered and who can say it is less mysterious than the mystery of personal survival? Indeed, the collection of molecules changes – completely every seven years or so, and partly as you read this page – so how are 'you' related to this changing molecular pile? The sword that lops off personal survival might lop off also personal existence now. The more perceptive Humanists see this dilemma, and also a close relative which may be considered together with it.

## Scientific language and freedom

Are molecules free? No-one can say what any one particle will do. The 'laws' are statistical and say what a thousand may be expected to do. But the numbers involved are so large that scientists can make definite pre-

[5] A. Flew in a review of T. R. Miles, *Eliminating the Subconscious* in *Humanist*, January 1967.
[6] A. J. Ayer (ed.), *The Humanist Outlook*, p. 259.

dictions and statements. The blood *will* do so and so; this drug *will* stimulate the brain in such and such a way. For every state of anger, love, hate, fear, vision, hearing, there is a pattern of excitement and chemical activity in the brain, nerves, bloodstream, *etc.* Where will my supposed freedom of action, my striving to overcome fear, my enjoyment of love, be found? Am I in fact shown up as a mere puppet, a ghastly molecular joke, thinking I choose when in fact the molecules are just performing their ordered and predictable dance? The observer who sticks electrodes into my brain, or checks my blood, will be able to say what I will do next. Is there even any sense in saying 'I' do it?

Of course this seems a silly conclusion. I *know* I choose and it's stupid to quibble over it. Many Humanists dismiss the matter – too easily perhaps because it lies near the root of their most cherished presuppositions. Those who put their trust in science should see what lord they have. It may be a good stick to beat 'superstitious' Christians with but what if it looks like beating freedom too?

The Communist – or part of him – is quite at home here. He is a materialist, even though a dialectical one, and hence all can be explained from matter. All social structures, economic systems, class-struggles follow their built-in laws. The process of thesis-antithesis-synthesis grinds relentlessly on. Determinism is king, from the dance of the molecules to the behaviour of nations. 'The socialist system will eventually replace the capitalist system; this is an objective law independent of man's will.'[7]

One or two Humanists have seen the point – that determinism rules out real personhood – and have even considered a temporary alliance with Christians to meet it. Nigel Bruce, reviewing Professor Halmos's book *The Faith of the Counsellors* (and there are many Humanists among the counsellors), writes:

[7] Mao Tse-tung at the fortieth anniversary of the October Revolution.

'The reason why counsellors find themselves uncomfortably poised is that they have one foot on medical ground and the other on the less substantial ground of individual psychology. They are treating their clients as individuals worthy of respect, capable of willpower, gifted with reason. But may not an increase in knowledge show that this is mere mysticism and that all the working of the individual person – intellectual, emotional and conative, as well as physical – are explicable in terms of physiology and biochemistry and are capable of being influenced by physiological and biochemical stimuli far more effectively than by personal counselling or by individual or group psychotherapy?

Are the counsellors, in fact, the last gasp of human idealism before we are submerged by an irresistible materialistic tide? Here we are again face to face with the appalling issue of *Brave New World* and *1984*.

Notice that, if this is to become a major threat to the Humanist position, as the social sciences advance Humanists will find themselves fighting on the same side as the better type of Christian. The Humanist's belief in the value of the individual is as fundamental to his outlook as it is to that of the genuine Christian. As long as this belief appears to be not inconsistent with scientific knowledge we can afford to put the main weight of our effort into issues on which we differ from the Christian Churches. But are we perhaps approaching a time when the discoveries of physiologists and biochemists will force us to make an agonising reappraisal of the Humanist attitude towards the individual? Shall we discover that, as Christians often tell us, Humanism still contains a large element of Christian idealism for which there is no scientific support?'[8]

[8] *Humanist*, May 1966.

## Complementary, not 'nothing but'

The freedom-determinist argument is, in one sense, old hat to Christians. They have been tossing predestination to and fro for centuries; without a lot of success, it may be said, and with the comforting safety-net that 'God's ways are past finding out'. When the ground shifts from celestial book-keeping to hard events in the everyday world they have found things more difficult. It's not just talking to fellow-believers – though that's hard enough – but trying to explain to others as well. Christians have had a bit of practice at this in discussing miracles, both in the Gospel stories and today (when Christian conversion at least warrants the term). At first God was a 'god of the gaps', a cosmic mechanic who leapt in to adjust the machinery at appropriate moments. As science explained more and more the gaps became fewer and fewer. God was in danger of becoming, as Huxley said, the smile on a cosmic Cheshire cat.

A different approach was tried and received some publicity in the 1950s. This approach isolated the snake in the verbal grass as the phrase 'nothing but'. To say that an event was 'nothing but' certain physical happenings might be too little. For example, the writing on the board is chalk. There is nothing but chalk there, each little bit in a position that can be accurately described and measured. But the message is obtained, not by listing the positions of all the bits of chalk, but by looking at it from a different viewpoint – not the scientific viewpoint of the describer of chalk particles, but the personal viewpoint of the reader who expects chalk marks to convey meaning.

So John Brown's body, even before it was mouldering in the grave, could be investigated chemically, but that did not exhaust all that could be known of John Brown. There was 'nothing but' chemicals, but by changing the viewpoint you met, not molecules milling about, but John Brown walking, talking and generally stirring things up politically. Nothing that you said about the chemistry affected the true statements about John Brown walking and talking. Nothing you said about John Brown walking and talking stopped the molecules doing their stuff. Not John Brown smuggled into gaps in the chemicals, but John Brown *and* the chemicals, both true. This might, incidentally, make it a bit easier to accept the mouldering-in-the-grave/marching-on idea.

A lot has been written about this 'complementary' view or 'multi-dimensional' view, as it is sometimes called. It clearly stopped the contention that science had driven God out. It showed that 'God-talk' and 'molecule-talk' were logically separate areas of discourse. The same argument would stop 'personal-talk' being reduced to 'molecule-talk'.

There is evidence that some Humanists have seen the relevance of complementarity as a buttress against reducing all to deterministic biochemistry. Julian Huxley wrote in 1961:

'We must beware of reductionism. It is hardly ever true that something is "nothing but" something else. Because we are descended from anthropoid primates, it does not follow that we are nothing but developed apes: because we are made of matter, it does not follow that we have nothing but material properties. An organization is always more than the mere sum of its elements, and must be studied as a unitary whole as well as analysed into its component parts.'[9]

In a paper presented to the Fourth Congress of the International Humanist and Ethical Union in 1966 Herbert Feigl spelt out in some detail the dangers of the 'reductive fallacy'. 'No Humanist is a materialist in the sense that he considers human values and ideals as sheer illusions' though he spoilt it by saying at the end,

[9] *The Humanist Frame*, p. 37.

'Human values and ideals are indeed the product of natural biological, psychological and social evolution'.[1] More recently E. H. Hutten has written of science and art as 'complementary ways of looking at man'.[2]

But the message is imperfectly received. Margaret Knight, in a contribution to a sixth-form general studies textbook, does not appear to understand the force of the argument. She dismisses Donald MacKay's use of the principle of complementarity: 'The most that can be said for it from the believer's point of view is that it provides a reply (though a weak one) to a particular argument against theism – namely the argument that scientific knowledge makes it unnecessary to give animistic explanations of natural events.' Yet on the previous page she accepts, in another context, that two explanations are different, but they do not conflict. 'Both are true, but neither is the whole truth. And the two together give a more complete picture of the situation than either alone.'[3]

It may be helpful to spell out in more detail what is involved in the reductive fallacy, because it dogs the argument at many points. A building is three-dimensional, but you cannot attend to all three dimensions at once. For many purposes it is useful to reduce it to a two-dimensional plan, elevation, *etc.* Such a reduction is useful and essential if lengths and angles are to be correctly shown. But to say that the house was 'only' the plan or elevation would be nonsense and create endless confusion and contradiction. Similarly, a sonata written for a full orchestra could be arranged and performed on a piano. This would be a reduction, but it would give some idea of the sonata. No-one who understood music would pretend it gave the 'full' or 'real' thing.

So with language. Human experience is full, 'solid', requiring different sorts of language to do justice to it –

[1] Reported in *Humanist*, November 1966.
[2] *Humanist*, May 1971.
[3] J. Brierley (ed.), *Science in its Context* (Heinemann, 1964), pp. 133, 132.

the descriptive language of science; the personal language of choice and awareness; the language of relationships and duty; the language of ultimate significance, religious truth and value. To suppose that you have said all there is to say about an experience when you have given an account in only one language is the reductive fallacy. The fuller, richer languages are reduced to one, partial account.

The road to reductionism is broad and slippery. Humanists should be pressed to consider this; partly to get a firmly logical basis for their undoubted belief that man is more than molecules, and partly because the door this opens leads to other rooms as well.

## One part of being human

At least this is a start. 'Molecules makyth man.' For some purposes we are machines, which a doctor can mend because he knows how they work. Our brain processes *are* like computer operations and there is no reason to suppose a complete account of all events concerning us cannot be given in mechanistic terms. This is what Laplace meant when he said of God, 'I have no need of that hypothesis.' As an observer describing the motions of the planets all he needed was the laws expressed by his equations. $\nabla^2 \phi = 0$ is true for atheist, Christian, Buddhist or Hindu. But that shows only how limited scientific enquiry is. A lot of interesting questions, such as How did matter begin? Why does it seem so wonderful? Are human beings significant? or How should we treat each other? cannot be answered in these terms.

The reaction to this view of man need not be an anxious squirm by Christians trying to drag God in, nor a fatalistic helplessness that it's all fixed and I can't really *do* anything. The mature attitude for Christian and Humanist is wonder and reverence – and for the Christian a step further to worship. 'I will praise thee, for I am fearfully and wonderfully made.'

# 2 Naked ape

### 'Life' is more than chemicals

The last chapter left out a most important observation. Even if the chemist could get the bits together in the right order, would he then have a man or a corpse? Weigh John Brown before and after death and there's no difference, but something's 'gone'. What is life? Do you add it? Or create it? Or perhaps just conserve it? The sperm is living when it fertilizes the ovum. Perhaps life is just passed on and the only other thing anyone can do is to kill it. Life is certainly mysterious. Its extraordinary persistence fascinates. Seeds found in a pharaoh's tomb germinated after more than 2,000 years' dry wait. No wonder the cycle of birth, growth, decay and death has been a major theme of human meditation and got itself mixed up in all sorts of religions as well.

The Humanist, as we have seen, wastes no time asking where matter came from, but he is less reticent about the origin of life. For him evolution explains all. 'Life evolved from non-living matter' is scattered through the literature. Evidence is scarce and attempts to make similar jumps from non-living to living in laboratory experiments are, to say the least, modest by comparison with the jump supposedly made in primaeval times which they have to corroborate. There are other, more difficult hurdles to clear as life becomes more complex. Victor Pearce[1] likens the enterprise to making a machine

[1] E. K. Victor Pearce, *Who was Adam?* (Paternoster, 1969). See chapter XIII, 'The impasse for "origin of life" biologists'.

tool factory when you haven't any tools to start with. Only slowly do we grasp the enormity of the jump, and the glib phrase, 'Life evolved from non-living matter' skips across the page too quickly to let people ponder. Evolution of the living is a bold enough hypothesis on its own; to extend it to jump the wider gap shows heroic or reckless faith. The grandeur of the concept may sweep all before it, or perhaps it commends itself to the Humanist mind only because, as Spencer put it, 'the alternative, special creation, is clearly incredible'.

No Christian was there to say it didn't happen that way. But they do little good by turning pseudo-scientist and reviling the evolutionists. Genesis 1 contains the profound statement that life characteristics are genetically transmitted – the earth put forth vegetation, plants yielding seed; the water brought forth swarms of living creatures to be fruitful and multiply and fill the waters. All is ascribed to God's creation without saying just how he did it or how long it took. There is a wide (and acrimonious) literature on the subject, in which both 'sides' have slips of insecurity showing and tend to slang each other rather than join in common wonder at a mystery neither can explain. Words are ill-defined, and Humanist writing is often hard pressed to keep to the purely descriptive, non-personal level. We find nature getting a capital N, and evolution a capital E as though 'they' (quasi-personalized) *did* something. Huxley actually calls his philosophy 'Evolutionary Humanism'. Evolution which started humbly as a working hypothesis for biologists gets somehow transmuted to an almost personal force behind all human development. From this it might be only a small step to the deterministic spirit of history which the Marxist sees driving all before it in human affairs. Few Humanists support this, however, because here they are not in the unevidenced world of the past but the here and now where they are desperately anxious to conserve the human individual against outside pressures – including Marxist ones.

To see how impressive this vision of progress seems to Humanists, Christians might read Huxley's introductory essay to *The Humanist Frame*.

> 'Man therefore is of immense significance . . . He is a reminder of the existence, here and there, in the quantitative vastness of cosmic matter and its energy-equivalents, of a trend towards mind, with its accompaniment of quality and richness and existence: and, what is more, a proof of the importance of mind and quality in the all-embracing evolutionary process . . . Animals, plants and micro-organisms, they are all his cousins or remoter kin, all parts of one single branching and evolving flow of metabolizing protoplasm.'[2]

Rona Hurst's comment about the influence of the new ideas is also illuminating:

> ' . . . the churches were immediately up in arms. Any believer in the new doctrines was branded a heretic or an atheist, and it took a long time for it to be realized that the doctrine of creation by evolution from primeval simplicity to various levels of complexity is far more inspiring than the idea of special creation, and is likely to evoke a deeper religious feeling in those who accept and understand it.'[3]

Again Christian apologists have argued that such bold design requires a Designer – whether in the mediaeval Latin of Aquinas or the colourful 'Fact and Faith' films of the Moody Institute of Science. Both invite us to reject the idea that the extraordinary phenomena of living things just happened. Humanists turn a deaf ear, and long ago found the loopholes in the argument from design which make it less than a logical certainty. For them there is no designer, only a 'trend'; 'chance' and

[2] See *The Humanist Frame*, pp. 18, 19.
Rona Hurst, *The Loom of Life* (Pemberton, 1964), p. 6.

'randomness' have to do duty for 'God', though these words prove, upon analysis, to be just as difficult to handle as the despised religious vocabulary. The battlefield is littered with pamphlets and inconclusive arguments and the occasional loss of a scholarly reputation due to overstating a case. The man in the street, meanwhile, does not read the literature but has the vague idea that evolution has disproved the Bible and that Christians are liable to be scientifically behind the times.

Here, as elsewhere, it may be helpful to mention that Christians rarely need to oppose Humanists in positive statements; it is only when Humanists go on to denials that resistance is called for. To say 'the evidence could mean it happened like this' is one thing. To add 'and therefore there is no God behind it' is another. The truth of the first statement is something scientists of all faiths or none can talk about, but it has no logical connection with the second statement.

For better or worse, then, one way or another, man is alive, with sufficient similarities of bodily form and function to some animals to provoke at least curiosity and comparison.

## The 'man is an animal' view

In recent years, this evolutionary motif has given rise to an unexpected backlash. 'A strange and disconcerting reversal . . . appears to be going on,' writes Dr John Lewis,[4] a prominent Humanist anthropologist, 'a movement, loudly proclaiming that it is scientific, modern, ruthlessly rational, is sweeping Humanism away as a discredited superstition. Half a dozen fashionable cults, believed in by everyone but scientists themselves, *in the name of science*, seek to persuade us that "man is a beast of prey", that beneath the veneer of civilization man is incurably aggressive, that "the cave man within" is the essential human type.'

[4] *Humanist*, September 1968.

It might be thought obvious that if you cannot look up to see what your Creator intended you to be, then you would look back to see what your antecedents suggested you might be. And this is what happened. The 1960s saw the publication of three or four books[5] which assumed that the 'real' human nature would be found from an examination of animal and bird behaviour. The result was deeply pessimistic. Readers of extracts in the Sunday papers learned that man, the 'naked ape', is 'inescapably hostile and competitive' and that even his friendships and loves are rooted in aggression and territory-defence.

The boasted human advance to reason and self-control – the proud results of Huxley's psycho-social evolution – were brushed aside as trivial, a superficial veneer on deeper behaviour patterns genetically transmitted from our animal ancestors. It all sounded very scientific with a welter of data, observations about apes of all sorts and sizes, grey-lag geese and fighting fish. Their habits were bizarre and furious, related to survival and territory. The slide across to human behaviour seemed plausible when you thought how even the best behave under provocation and the 'underlying' aggression breaks through. Anthony Storr really laid it on thick in the introduction to his book *Human Aggression* (which he dedicates to Konrad Lorenz with 'admiration and affection', qualities which apparently temporarily overlaid his aggressive tendencies):

'That man is an aggressive creature will hardly be disputed . . . the cruellest and most ruthless species that has ever walked the earth; and that, although we may recoil in horror when we read in newspaper or history book of the atrocities committed by man upon man, we know in our hearts that each one of us har-

[5] Robert Ardrey, *The Territorial Imperative* (Collins, 1967); Desmond Morris, *The Naked Ape* (Cape, 1967; Corgi, 1969); Konrad Lorenz, *On Aggression* (Methuen, 1966); Anthony Storr, *Human Aggression* (Penguin, 1968).

bours within himself those same savage impulses which lead to murder, to torture and to war.'[6]

There is more than a suggestion in all this that aggression, like sexual impulse, is built into humanity by biological development and there is really little you can do about it. Storr suggested that competitive games offered one way of letting off steam, and behaviour at some football matches might bear this out. The thesis gained support, too, from Freud's ideas of aggressive instincts, too powerful to be crushed, too uncertain to be sublimated, lurking repressed in the subconscious. On this view the programme for living that is being fed into every human computer is not a pleasant one, but we may as well know the worst and not kid ourselves that moral exhortation and good resolve are going to change things much.

Meanwhile, back at the literary ranch, William Golding's novel *Lord of the Flies* was being turned into a blood-curdling film. Wrecked on a remote island, a group of decent, middle-class boys do not react with *Coral Island* peace and ingenuity but become violently divided, killing and destroying in their hate and terror. His novel *The Inheritors* helped on the aggressive image. The 'Theatre of Cruelty' churned out plays to shock audiences with the depths of human wickedness. TV brought us daily its pictures of war in Vietnam, and its up-to-the-minute record of horror and atrocity from all over the world. It looked as if Robert Ardrey was right: 'nations as well as animals obey the laws of the territorial imperative'.

### Criticism of 'Naked Ape'

Christians may perhaps have got a little illicit pleasure from this fresh awareness that 'the heart is desperately corrupt' but the main leap to the defence of man came from the Humanist camp. Dr John Lewis, in the article already quoted, took three of the offending authors soundly to task. Later, he and a Roman Catholic

[6] Anthony Storr, *Human Aggression*, p. 9.

anatomist, Bernard Towers, produced a powerful demolition of Desmond Morris's book under the title *Naked Ape or Homo Sapiens?*[7] Among other things they argued that human body hair is not so easily dismissed as Morris's word 'naked' implies, and also that humans missed the 'ape' bus long ago, being descended from a much earlier branch of the genealogical tree. But in two important chapters they denounce the 'nothing-buttery' of the instinct-merchants and conclude:

'It is therefore quite mistaken to explain man in terms of the built-in reactions of animals lacking in the capacity to plan their actions on the bases of elaborate roundabout methods and tools requiring intelligence, foresight, imagination and planning. An animal has none of these capacities. He lives entirely in the present, as all animal psychology insists.'

And later they acknowledge 'leaps' in the evolutionary programme:

'We do not say that life is *only* chemistry, and we do not say that mind is *only* the activity of cortical neurones; just as we do not say that man is *only* an ape. We recognize the emergence of the entirely new.'[8]

So they go on to deal with the uniqueness of man. Far from being overawed by his similarity to animals, we should rejoice in the powers of mind and planning which he alone enjoys. The Towers-Lewis partnership itself is evidence that Christians and Humanists can agree about that, though they might have different ideas on how the 'leap' or 'emergence' should be accounted for.

Humanists hastened to add that we need not fear that any religious idea of original sin was being smuggled in.

[7] John Lewis and Bernard Towers, *Naked Ape or Homo Sapiens?* (Garnstone Press, 1969). This is in the Teilhard Library series and it is interesting to see a Humanist contributing. They are not usually impressed with de Chardin's brand of evolutionism as it seems to have too many religious strings attached.
[8] *Op. cit.*, pp. 62, 71.

Indeed, in a lecture, Dr Lewis likened Morris's book to the scientific equivalent of the Christian doctrine of original sin which would be equally debilitating. Margaret Knight went further and set out to show that beasts aren't all that beastly. There were impulses to co-operation and kindness as well, as Darwin had said:

'The social instincts – the prime principle of man's moral constitution – with the aid of active intellectual powers and the effects of habit, naturally lead to the golden rule, "As ye would that men should do to you, do ye also to them likewise." '

She adds:

'The crucial point in the present context is that co-operation and aggression are biologically on a level. Both have survival value; both are built-in; both manifest themselves spontaneously in appropriate circumstances. This, basically, is the humanist position, and it contrasts sharply with the traditional Christian view, as will later be shown.'

Christians may as well know how Humanists (or one Humanist) sees them:

'The widespread Christian hostility to Humanism is probably due largely to the belief that it undermines the basis of morals. Humanists, however, are disposed to reverse the argument. They maintain that the Christian ethic is basically defective, in that it has, so to speak, stood natural morality on its head; it has denied and discouraged man's natural social tendencies, and encouraged a self-centred preoccupation with one's own virtue and one's own salvation.'[9]

## But still more to being human
This is certainly more than molecules. To be human is to be alive, to have capacities of mind, action and reaction, as well as an underworld of impulses, aggressions and drives.

[9] A. J. Ayer (ed.), *The Humanist Outlook*, pp. 49, 50.

Can we be clearer about this? Humanists may have got mankind off the Morris-Lorenz hook but have they made it clear just what this human power is that governs impulses? Margaret Knight almost suggests that social and anti-social instincts ('biologically on a level') are built in and show through in living willy-nilly. Does this again dispose of 'me' living my life and deciding what sort of person I shall be? If not, the mechanism of control is imperfectly described and there is all too much room for the human person to slip through the impulsive net and get lost. The way is also horribly open for anyone, from brainwashers to subliminal advertisers, to get working on my impulses and do what they want with me.

On the other side, have Christians got original sin mixed up with inherited aggressions? It is clear Humanists think so and have not got much of a picture of the Christian view of man. Perhaps Christians have been too ready to spring up shouting 'I told you so' at every demonstration of hate or cruelty; too ready to dismiss the social case-worker's account of contributory factors as 'just excuses'. Perhaps Humanists are anxious to find 'excuses' lest their bold picture of man's march to maturity be spoilt. Both 'sides' have scope for explanation and elucidation. Christians must make it clear that sexual and aggressive impulses are not sin; not even wrong. They are part of the human equipment as much as the cells and nerves. Wrongdoing starts only when the elusive 'I' starts using the equipment, directing it to 'my' rather than others' interests. Humanists and Christians can be agreed on this. But they part company when the Christian points out that such actions are not only wrong but sinful, *i.e.* my wrongdoing is not just something between myself and my fellow-humans but between myself and God. 'Against thee, thee only, have I sinned. . . . ' But that is a long way further on yet. For the moment, being human is more than just chemicals or naked-apery. But the 'more' needs to be spelt out more clearly.

33

# 3 Economic man

## Man the tool–maker

If you find remains in a cave, how do you decide whether they represent man or animal? Since some famous finds are just a jaw-bone or shoulder-blade you'll need either good imagination or more evidence. The evidence often turns out to be fragments of tools, flint axes, ornaments, or ashes. Minimal man is a tool-maker. He goes to work on his environment and uses tools to increase his power.

At a less minimal level, he becomes the settled farmer, learning to hoe and sow, to reap and mow, as well as to practise animal husbandry. A stage or two later he shows traces of trade; barter and subsistence economy at first, and then the sophistication of cash economy and all the modern paraphernalia of commerce and big business.

Anthropologists have got it all logged up. Flint tools date early man. Pottery dates later finds. With extraordinary skill and patience the clues are fitted together so that you can almost imagine yourself living in Neolithic villages of 10,000 BC or the more recent glories of Mycenae.

Try your hand at making a flint axe sometime – it will take some time, too. Try your hand at making a gold mask like the finds at Argos. Here is something distinctively human. Here are skills to use the world, to turn it to advantage for food and (more surprisingly) for enjoyment and beauty.

A major part of the description of any society is its

economic effort, the things it produces, the techniques it uses. Marxists see a progress in the means of production and exchange. Economic systems follow laws like everything else. Most sociologists seem to agree some of the time, though they don't like the deterministic bit and spend the rest of their time urging people to be aware of, to resist or change the present economic system.

Human skill has almost worked itself out of some jobs, by inventing machines to do them. Often the machines do the jobs more quickly, more accurately, more reliably than men could and produce so much more that another important human activity appears.

## Producer and consumer

The human being becomes the 'consumer'. Advertisements assure him he must have what the machines pour out. And having bought it, he must get through it, to be ready for the next lot. Use, use, use – or if you can't use, throw it away. So we become what Vance Packard called 'The Waste Makers'.

In recent years the picture of economic man, producer and consumer, has attracted a lot of attention, not least from Christians and Humanists. It is, of course, not a universal phenomenon and writers hasten to show that consumption is no problem in India. Bellies in Bihar can cope easily with the occasional meal they get. But even here the thinking is often economically motivated, as though compassion and duty were insufficient goads to action. Idle starving Indians, we are reminded, are not producing all they could, nor soaking up the factory produce they might do if they worked and earned. Hence the producer-consumer view of man colours thinking deeply.

Is this the ideal man? What shall we say about the current economic yardstick? It has built-in measures of success. Countries are arranged in a league table by average earnings or Gross National Product. The successful man is the man who makes two lathes work where one worked before, or designs one lathe to do the work of two. It has the same fascination in its own way as the dance of the molecules. The complexity of machinery and administration which runs a modern insurance office, with a computer that churns out 100 tons of paperwork a week; the precision of a car assembly plant making a car a minute; that technological show-piece, a space-vehicle in orbit round the moon – these put man well above the chemicals and impulse class.

Also, we are told, the drudgery goes out of work. Thousands of labourers with pick and shovel built the British railways. The new motorways are done by far fewer, far more skilled workers with bulldozers and mountain-movers. Motorways for newer, faster cars, made by newer, faster equipment in bigger and better factories.

And yet – is this the height of human achievement? The bookish tend to be above the sweat of the factory floor or transport driver's cab. They write learnedly to each other about economic systems, but occasionally spare the odd thought for what all this producing and consuming has made of man. It may be significant that *The Humanist Outlook* contains no essay specifically about this, though the plight of under-developed countries gets good coverage. Perhaps they are so occupied with macro-economics, the wide sweep of social patterns and re-forms, that they don't come across the producer-consumer in the street. Christians have traditionally had a theology of work, but it has only recently had much of an airing. The field is wide open for a fresh look at economic man. He may focus attention on some of the presuppositions of both Christians and Humanists.

# Dangers of the economic view of man

## *1. Impersonal*

The reference to 'wide view' brings to mind at once a less pleasant fact about economic man. He is impersonal and comes in statistical packets. One million housewives use Fizz or Whizz. An advertising campaign changes 20,000 to Fazz or Whazz. A new factory will give 1,000 jobs. The computer rolls out statistics about population movements, labour mobility coefficients and output per head. Wage rates are negotiated for 'x thousand operatives'. If only producing and consuming matter, are we concerned just who does it? One thousand people buying Brand X in Y's supermarket can be old, young, criminal, ugly or saintly, as long as they pay up at the check-out.

Traffic control wizards count cars and draw flow charts. New one-way systems or lights make thousands of people obediently change their routes, stop the city streets snarling up, or delay the need for the new by-pass for a year or two. At the holiday season, food supplies are re-routed to cater for the thousands in their unaccustomed seaside habitats. It's all reminiscent of the ant-hill, or 'city of the bees'. Not quite so efficient yet, nor so relentless, but highly organized with the help of statistics which say what 'man' on average will do, kept going mainly by profit motive, high-pressure advertising, and an army of planners, many of whom are honestly trying to 'do the best for people' in an overcrowded environment.

Everybody does their own bit, amplified a hundred-fold by machinery, so that goods, cars, holidays are more available than ever before. The 'division of labour' which has so revolutionized production may have some doubtful accompaniments (which we may look at later) but it has very literally produced the goods. In Britain we may be thankful that standards of living once available only to the rich are now open to nearly all. We may, however, still wonder if men and women are getting lost in 'man'.

Again, considering a wider view, 'man' seems lop-sided. When Neil Armstrong described the first step on the moon as 'a big step forward for mankind', what 'man' did people understand? Newspaper correspondence columns sprang to violent life. Ought so much to be spent on moon research when half the world was starving? They concluded that the space programme was in fact only a small part of the Gross National Product of the nations involved – that they could irrigate India *as well* if they wanted to – but still the gap between the highly educated, technological wizards of Houston, USA, and the South American peasant using his primitive farming methods, is a wide one. Trevor Huddleston writes movingly of the tension he felt when he heard, over a radio in a Masai village, the voice of the first man in space.[1]

Optimists often write as if moon landings show what 'man' is capable of, and as if the sorting out of earthly troubles is only a matter of time. The man in the street stolidly doubts it, though he may not think his doubt through as clearly as some novelists have done for him. What happens to the individual or local group when 'man' controls the universe? The super-planners, the highly intelligent, the tycoons, press on their way and blaze new trails. Everyone can see how clever and valuable they are. Their achievements fill TV screens all over the world. But what about the ordinary chap, producing his daily quota and consuming his daily share? How significant is he, and to whom? Does he exist just for the great human machine, to keep the ant-hill going? And if the managers decide he could do it better in some other way, they have all the techniques available, from statutory orders to biological engineering. *Brave New World*, with its dating from AF, the Year of our

[1] Trevor Huddleston, *The True and Living God* (Fontana, 1964).

38

Ford, is more possible now than when Aldous Huxley wrote it. We are not so far from pharaoh's pyramid-building schemes as we may like to think. Economic man raises his standard of living and his susceptibility to exploitation and direction at about the same rate.

## 2. Christian and Humanist reaction

What have Christians and Humanists to say about this 'Man or man?' question? Christians can rejoice in Man's achievement. 'What is man?' asks the psalmist, and finds his greatest wonder in 'thou hast made him' and 'thou hast given him dominion'. Man mirrors the creative and controlling power of God and extends his dominion over the earth entrusted to him. Collectively men do all these things and show cause for the tribute of praise: 'How majestic is thy name in all the earth!' But groups and individuals are equally known to God, whether the chosen nation, the nations round about, the exploiting landowner or the poor man or widow who cries in the Psalms for judgment. Even the slave is ennobled to be the Lord's freeman and 'to serve the Lord Christ'. The slave-economy, as opponents do not hesitate to say, is not attacked very hard in the New Testament, but each believer may know the liberty of being the son of his heavenly Father. A liberty open to all, unlike the division Aristotle made – mechanics and artisans probably had no leisure to think their way to the good life; slaves certainly couldn't and must be kept going with punishments and rewards.

Humanists glory in man's achievements. Man is the master of things. In spite of set-backs and appalling tasks still to be done (often blamed on Christian reaction and other-worldliness in the past) the optimistic forward march looks possible yet. They profess great concern for the individual, too. They object to a 'Closed Society' because it hampers individual growth, and press for an 'Open Society' in which public means are available for private ends and in which men and women can show diversity and personal preference. Their writings show little detailed working out of this at the level of economic man doing his eight hours a day. But the 'public means' depend to a great extent on the benefits of mass production, social guidance, health and welfare services, often manned by specialists. The producer-consumer image is little modified, with little indication why the ordinary chap – who isn't making evident contributions to 'man's achievements' – is significant.

### 3. Replaceable units

Another depressing feature of economic man is his replaceability. If George has an accident, another welder can be found. If half a dozen go on strike, the work can be sent elsewhere. Ships have even been known to be towed to Rotterdam for fitting out when a British yard couldn't guarantee a finish on time. Flood or famine may wipe out half a million consumers in Bangladesh, but new markets boom elsewhere. Even professional jobs have this unhappy feature. My own most pressing experience of it occurred when a well-respected school colleague collapsed and died in ten minutes. I had to take time off from grief to arrange reliefs for his classes and think about advertising for a replacement. The human ant-hill keeps going. Is it all there is?

### 4. The old and the handicapped

There are a few exceptions to the producer-consumer picture. Children, of course, but then they are being trained to be the producers and – most important of all, it seems – the consumers of the future. The old stay old longer as medical science improves. Many of them are still in the ranks of the consumers, spending what they saved during their productive years. Other elderly folk were once valued for the experience and wise counsel they offered. Now increasingly they become 'problems'.

But the exceptions are not all old. A holiday each year with a group of spastic young people impresses this deeply. Brain damage has impaired speech or movement. Some learn to adapt well enough to integrate with society and hold down a normal job. In years gone by the survival rate was much lower, but now many live on in homes and institutions, sometimes unable to do anything at all economically significant. Economically in fact, they are a drain upon society, consuming little themselves but necessitating considerable expense in buildings, trained helpers and services. What is 'human' for these young people? As economic men they don't qualify and yet to spend a fortnight with them is to find deep and often mature humanity, capacity for thought, appreciation, humour, anxiety and hope. They have skills, like typing laboriously with stick in mouth, or turning pages of a book with their toes, but these skills are not marketable. They need, not pity, but understanding, and this is difficult in a society which has so few criteria to estimate human worth except financial ones. Several find added significance and purpose in their Christian faith, and have said that bitterness and confusion have receded and fresh opportunities of thought and relationship followed their awareness of a relationship with Christ.

There seems little Humanist writing devoted to these non-producers, though many Humanist students and others show kindness and spend time with handicapped people. Sometimes such people explode with frustration, angrily enquiring of the Christians why their God allows such things. More generally they patiently get on with what help they can, encouraging interest and such activity as is possible. Can they go beyond this? What significance can they offer? Humanists write, quite properly, on abortion and euthanasia and talk of the evil of life that has no human dignity. But what gives life dignity when the ready-made criteria of producer-consumer are not applicable? One of my handicapped friends refers to himself and those like him as 'the thinkers' and to the rest of us as 'the doers'. Time was when people withdrew from society to devote themselves to meditation and religious exercises. They were (and are) reviled as unproductive. The monasteries combined religious leisure with painstaking and enlightened labour in field and hospital. But the modern consumer-producer seems to be the subject of a conspiracy. When he isn't producing he is consuming, if it's only petrol and the batteries of the transistor that goes everywhere with him. Ironically, the vastly increased 'leisure' has given rise to new industries – tourist, sporting, holiday, hobbies – whose services and goods are consumed by the leisured.

## Human is more than economics

Human skill, inventiveness and productiveness are certainly part of the story. But the trade and production statistics do not show everything. There are many who find genuine enjoyment in work and in using the labours of others, and many whose leisure is purposeful and fulfilling. Men do not live by bread alone – though Christians and Humanists will differ on the rest of that saying. 'The functionalist view of man', wrote Gabriel Marcel, 'involves a degradation of the human person.' That is the Existentialist protest in every age. It's *I* who matter, not just what I do in the system. Humanist and Christian would agree. But how is the functionalist view to be resisted? How can its fallacy be exposed? What *is* a person beyond a functional unit of society?

# 4 Me

## A new language

The chemist can make his description. He uses verbs in the indicative mood to say what 'is', what the molecules 'do'. The psychologist describes the impulses and complexes and says how they determine behaviour. The commercial statistics give full description of productive and consuming patterns. So they build up a picture of me by which I can be recognized by observers. I can adopt a detached attitude and talk the same language. Some people do. 'I am well aware of my prejudices', they say, 'and try to think objectively about each situation.'

This observer language (the 'molecule-talk' of p. 11) might conceivably one day be expanded to include all events, looked at from this viewpoint. But if you try, just for an hour, to restrict yourself to this vocabulary, you will find it very difficult, and also rather dull, because the more interesting things you want to say have to be cut out.

Frequent reference has been made to men and women being 'more than' a certain description, more than just molecules, chemicals, animals or workers. The 'more' needs a different language to describe it. Some words may be the same but they will have different force. For example, when the observer says, 'John knows Jill is ill, so he'll probably go and see how she is', 'knows' is a shorthand for information in a memory store (like a computer's data bank), 'will probably' is the statistical result from lots of information about John's reactions to Jill in the past, and the data bank's records of how similar situations have worked out in the past. If, in fact, John doesn't go, the memory store logs up one more incident which will help the calculation of probability next time. The observer might also be able to predict certain physical signs of anxiety, based on what is known of John's actions in the past and the actions of people in similar situations. But to John, 'I know Jill is ill' is a complex human experience involving anxiety, hope, maybe irritation that he'll have to cancel the weekend party, *etc*.

'Mary is angry with Peter' is observer shorthand for a lot of physiological sensations and impulsive reactions. To Mary it is experienced as an emotional matter mixed up with value judgments of justification or shame. This personal language (or 'me-talk') is not a rival or contradictory account of what the observer describes in 'molecule-talk'. Both accounts can be true and neither can be reduced to the other. The observer cannot say that John's anxiety is *only* (or *really*) an automatic response to the stimulus of Jill's illness, nor can Jill say that her illness is 'only in the mind'. Both kinds of language are necessary, each respecting its proper limits.

## The mystery of personal knowledge

This personal 'me-talk' is so familiar to us that we do not realize its mystery and marvels. It is only when you start writing computer programmes, for instance, that you realize how limited its language is, and how difficult it would be to tell it to do lots of things you do automatically. It will consult a million memory stores and tell you how many have the symbols that mean blue eyes, but how do you tell it to 'let me know when Jill comes in'? You would find it difficult, perhaps, to describe Jill exactly to the new typist, but she might make a reasonable guess as to her identity when she comes through the door. How do you recognize people? What clues tell you, and how do you fit the clues together? There may be a long and complicated 'molecule-talk' account of recognition, but in 'me-talk' it's a single experience, perhaps mingled with surprise or alarm or pleasure. The same is true of the experience of memory and forethought, with which hope is connected. This is what makes human 'fear' different from animal 'fright', and makes choosing a difficult and often exhausting matter.

Most surprising of all, perhaps, is conviction. The certainty of knowledge which is far more than ability to recall a statement from a memory store. Cybernetically the information may be linked with all sorts of other information, like the place and time I heard or read it, the tone of voice in which I was told, the things it fits with, the flash of recognition as I was aware of the fitting together. But all these bits somehow have a new pattern of certainty, just as the bits of paint on the canvas have a pattern which is the picture.

An extension of this makes it possible for me to think how other people feel – to sympathize and 'put myself in their position'. Most psychologists would say the uniqueness of man is tied up with his use of this language. Animals operate by instinct in the present; man thinks, timelessly.

This language plays tricks on us. If you look at it, it disappears. You tell me you enjoy a game of tennis. Now, supposing I happen to see you on court in mid-game and ask you at that point to tell me how you enjoy yourself. If you start analysing – the muscular exercise, the company, the pleasant air, the achievement of a good stroke, and so on – the enjoyment somehow slips through it all and you will very likely miss the next shot as well! Similarly if you analyse 'me-talk' you find you are making it something external to you. It becomes observer statements about how other people use words.

Michael Polanyi, successively Professor of Chemistry

45

and Philosophy at Liverpool University, has given a lot of attention to this elusive, personal knowledge.[1] It is best, he says, not to think of analogies with items of information passively stored in filing cabinets, but to think of knowing as a positive active process. He suggests that whenever we attend *to* something, we attend *from* something. Our active knowledge rests on an underlying presupposition. If we observe an experiment we are assuming there are causes and effects, and that we can understand how it works. Similarly if we read a letter we expect it to have meaning; if we weigh evidence we assume we have some capacity for thought and choice. These presuppositions *from* which we attend – which make it possible to attend *to* the matter in hand – he calls *tacit* knowledge. He thinks we are in danger of overlooking its existence just because we are not usually attending *to* it, but *from* it.

All this has been laboured because just here is a favourite bolt-hole or escape route of woolly thinking. Push some people hard enough about their personal awareness (especially, perhaps, about awareness of moral duty, guilt or God) and they will eventually slip into, 'Well it's your upbringing, or habit, or the book you've been reading, really.' (Always suspect that word 'really' – it's another way of saying 'nothing but'.) What they mean is that you can forget 'me-talk' – it's all 'molecule-talk' really. In other words they are *reducing* humanity by cutting out the human experiences that are expressed in personal language. And this often happens because, although they are aware of the presuppositions of 'molecule-talk' – cause and effect, and so on – they don't realize the presuppositions of 'me-talk' – awareness of responsibility, values, awe and wonder. These are *presuppositions*. They cannot be proved or disproved by scientific observation. They are the foundation of a different way of

[1] *E.g.* M. Polanyi, *The Tacit Dimension* (Routledge and Kegan Paul, 1967).

looking at experience. This gives rise to muddle. H. J. Blackham, for example, defines Humanism as, among other things, 'an assumption of responsibility for one's own life and for the life of mankind',[2] as if this was something rather special, a personal commitment. In one sense it might be, but the better word would then be 'recognition of responsibility . . . '. Responsibility in human parlance, is not more special than order, regularity, cause and effect are in observer language. These things are implicit in all scientists' talk about their experiments; and responsibility is implicit in all personal language about living, choosing, acting. The Christian view is that man *is* responsible, whether he makes the assumption or not, and that his language betrays him as more than animal, more than observer, a *person* who can be called to account, not only by his own choice or conscience, but by God.

## Identity crisis: do I really exist?

But the sharp edges of responsibility have been blurred. The springs of language have been muddied with over-emphasis upon observer talk and analysis. Emotion and feeling, especially if connected with duty, have all too often been hastily explained away by reduction to molecule-talk. No wonder that sometimes young people are overwhelmed. The molecule account, or the impulse or economic account, seems so buttoned up, so closely knit that there isn't any more to be said. A man will suddenly conclude that all he does and thinks can be accounted for in terms of genes or environment: he is small, insignificant and replaceable; he therefore sees little point in his bit of the ant-hill. Few people would care if he died and those few would soon get over it. Hence the cry, 'Who am I?', 'Do I matter?', or the suicide note when some final straw tips the balance: 'There's no point in living any more.' The Open Society,

[2] H. J. Blackham, *Humanism*, p. 13.

for which Humanists press, is likely to produce more of these crises – a fact which Professor A. J. Ayer, a former president of the BHA, points out in his essay in *Towards an Open Society*.[3] The Closed Society contained lots of guidelines, measures, status, supports, many of which cramped personal development. As these go, people will need greater conviction of personal responsibility and significance if they are to survive the identity crisis.

The treatment of this crisis is not by talk alone – though explanation of languages may help at some stage. The 'patient' will have to be helped to *live as though he mattered*; to attend to life from the assumption of personhood; to look for personal relationships; to expect personal involvement, enjoyment, pain, duty and due; to remember that the impersonal explanations that keep springing to mind are only *one* way – and not the most interesting or important way – of talking about things. There is at least this personal way – and Christians believe there is a further way in which we can talk about our responsibility to God and his care of us.

Because molecules, impulses and economic circumstances differ, each of us brings different equipment to the job of being human. Reaction to experience varies so that we build up different characters and habits. Humanists often speak of 'fulfilment' as a goal and they want society organized as far as possible to allow this to the greatest possible number of people, so that each one can develop his capacities and take full advantage of his opportunities. This will concern us more in detail when we come to consider relationships in society, but for the moment, note that 'fulfilment' is not just doing whatever you want, following impulses of hunger, sex, or violence. 'Fulfilment' is subtler and in fact smuggles in a host of value judgments. It comes to mean 'become the best person you are capable of becoming'. Use your opportunities, but in such a way that they harmonize, that

[3] William Purcell (ed.), *Towards an Open Society* (Pemberton, 1971).

there are no inner tensions, no uncontrolled impulse, but that you become a 'whole person'. Realize that *you* are acting; take responsibility for the sort of person you are becoming. Don't slide out of it with 'molecule-talk' ('I can't help it, it's my genes and hormones'), but recognize what equipment you've got and determine to make the best of it.

This is a noble ideal – a little vague in that 'best' is not defined – and as long as it stays positive, Christians can go along with it happily. They will feel something important is lost if Humanists go negative and say 'but of course you're on your own, so there's no God-awareness to develop, and no capacity to fulfil for worship of anything greater than Man'.

## The relationship between me and nature

Nature, for this purpose, is 'how things are', the way the molecules, *etc*. work, the things I describe in molecule-talk. Man (with a capital M) is controlling some of this, making deserts blossom, finding drugs to cure disease, and so on. There are a few modest ways in which *I* can control it, like putting up an umbrella in the rain or taking codeine for a headache. But since 'I' am different from nature, there is the possibility of reaction between nature and me. What shall that reaction be?

At one extreme is the 'one with nature' approach. It boils down to 'You're an animal really; so live like one. Just follow the impulses. Think with the blood.' This is repudiated by both Christian and Humanist as being less than fulfilment. We are 'more' than nature and can't give in as easily as that.

At the other extreme is the 'Get away from nature' approach. By asceticism or meditation, forget about the molecules; be pure idea, joined to the idea behind the molecules of nature. This is the Enlightenment of the East, and in the increasingly materialistic culture of the West it has at present a lot of attraction and not a few customers. H. J. Blackham will have none of it, partly because of its connection with what he terms 'the Perennial Philosophy':

'the immemorial view that recognizes in the human being an element of identity cognate with the Ground of all being, and the way of life which seeks the union or reunion of the detached and disciplined self with this Ground, of human being with being. The assumptions of the Perennial Philosophy in all its forms are contrary to the assumptions of humanism, and therefore it would seem that all these dependent disciplines and techniques of withdrawal and concentration are of no use nor interest to humanists. . . . . it would seem, techniques for living in the traditions of the East have no relevance to the modern west represented in humanism.'[4]

But he wants to find a 'safe' method of achieving the openness to the past, the fullness of experience and thought, that these disciplines claim to give.[5]

Christians have had their meditating mystics, but traditionally have been against trying to forget the molecules. Perennial Philosophy, yes, in so far as God is the Ground of Being and can be known. But he is known, not in spite of molecules and things, but *through* them.

So you can't beat nature and you mustn't join it. You have to live in tension. It can be creative tension. It could be diagrammatically expressed

$$\textbf{Me} \longleftrightarrow \textbf{Nature}$$

where the arrows represent me controlling nature and

[4] H. J. Blackham, *Humanism*, p. 71.
[5] Ronald Hepburn, however, in H. J. Blackham (ed.), *Objections to Humanism* (Constable, 1963; Penguin, 1965), p. 51, is less ready to abandon 'nature-mystical experiences . . . '. 'In the light of them, we can no longer see the world simply as our quarry, our rubbish tip, ours to consume or ravish or take as spoil.'

50

nature limiting me. 'Nature to me' includes its 'there-ness', its inescapability, its power, to all of which I may respond aesthetically, with awe, and with genuine appreciation of its beauty. There is tension here – the fear of the thunderstorm, but wonder at its power and the beauty of the lightning, the *numen*, fascinating and tremendous of which Otto wrote.[6] This can't be written off as just ignorance – the response of primitive man (however you define primitive). Knowing how lightning works doesn't stop scientists watching spell-bound – or even worshipping, for to many scientists, as to the Hebrew shepherd-king, 'The heavens are telling the glory of God; and the firmament proclaims his handiwork.'

Humanists don't go in for the last bit, but are good at appreciation of the beauty, power – and possibility – of nature.[7]

The arrows in the diagram may also include the delicate balance of accepting and striving with nature. Man (with capital M) may be wrestling with nature about cancer. Meanwhile I may be told I have two years to live. Spina bifida infants nowadays can get surgery that puts them over the stile and on the way to normal development, but some of my friends were born too early for this. They have to come to terms with nature as they find it now. I may leave no stone unturned to see what can be done for my rheumatism, but eventually have to settle that this *is* going to be a limitation I must live with. It is not nice to be limited and the impulsive reaction is to lash out in frustration. Bitterness arises which in turn makes it harder to act constructively and rationally. Humanists emphasize this, since rational action is their watchword. No doubt they can show evidence of people who have learned to make the accommodation. Many

[6] R. Otto, *The Idea of the Holy* (Penguin, 1959), chapter iv.
[7] See, *e.g.*, Ronald Hepburn in *Objections to Humanism*, p. 32, where he describes the 'numinous awe' of the scientist, but is at pains to show it is not the 'shudder or thrill of Job's or Isaiah's encounter with Yahweh'.

have borne pain and handicap with patience and dignity. Christians have often done so with the additional burden of answering the taunt, 'Where is your God now?' The achievement of many such is acclaimed as human greatness – the Helen Kellers, Louis Brailles and others who have done so much for themselves and others highlight the creative tension between 'me' and 'nature'.

## The 'I'm-in-charge' view

Here we may mention briefly a question which will need deeper treatment when we widen out from 'me' to 'us' and 'them'. In this tension with the world, is there any arbiter? Are no holds barred? If I am ill, is medicine my only aid – or may I also pray? May I control nature in any way I like, raping the earth and polluting it in any way that ministers to my immediate need? Is there any limit to the pain I may inflict on animals for my advantage – blood sports or vivisection? Humanists are against praying and pollution, and are probably about as divided on blood sports as most other people. Praying is not only against their presupposition of man on his own, but also seems, common-sensibly, to be beyond proof. Pollution, equally common-sensibly, seems 'wrong', and here some idea of responsibility to future generations – to Man with capital M – is often smuggled in.

The biblical view is that *the Lord God* put the man in the garden to till it and to dress it. He has dominion because it has been given him. He is, in Milton's words, 'the master work' who will

> ' . . . upright with front serene
> govern the rest, self-knowing, and from thence
> magnanimous, to correspond with Heaven.'[8]

Humanists of course reject this as a myth which they have outgrown. Man is now master and wants no God

[8] *Paradise Lost*, VII, 504.

telling him how to cope. Religious rituals may have had some use at one time, determining the cycle of sowing, reaping, conservation and sound breeding. But now men rule untrammelled. Not all Humanists are equally happy at this. A recent dialogue between Professor Edmund Leach and Theodore Roszak in the magazine *Humanist*[9] makes illuminating reading. Both contributors wish to avoid any reference to God, a real God who is there. Leach is all for men realizing their godhood and taking on the role, controlling everything without a look over the shoulder. Roszak, more feelingly – one is tempted to say 'more humanly' – wants to conserve the reverence. Humanism, he says, is Promethean, snatching the fire from the gods and taking what comes. In a final contribution, Roszak writes:

'I will not disrespect it, since I am also a child of that defiant firebringer . . . even though I realize that such filial loyalty may well be the death of us all. And yet, as Leach recognizes, the task is to resign the stolen fire . . . or some of it . . . I think *much* of it. Of course, of course. But how shall we pry that torch from the grip of these covetous hands? Myths of graceful renunciation are now what we need. And I fear it will not be the humanists who provide them. Humanism is theft of the fire, *not* repentance . . . let alone restoration . . . . I cannot think that pride will sacrifice power. Not really. Not for long. To pride, sacrifice is another inflation of the imperial ego . . . On the other hand, love casts out power gladly, like so much of a burden to its joys, knowing the great truth "All lose, Whole find". But love must have an object – which is not, like pride's, the reflection in one's mirror, the shadow at one's heel. And that object must live. It must be *seen* to live.'[1]

[9] *Humanist*, May, June, July, 1971.
[1] *Humanist*, July 1971, p. 212.

The problem, for Humanists, is to find such an object, an object that lives and commands love, and that is seen to live. Christians should learn to rejoice more in the God whose glory the heavens are telling, to share that joy in, and respect for, nature, that breathes in the Psalms, was embodied in St Francis, and has been the joy and inspiration of artist and worker, monk and layman, for centuries.

## A step nearer humanness

To be human, then, includes experiences that demand a whole new language. It involves a viewpoint that sets the person over against nature in a tension that can be creative and often painful, a tension that is all too readily snapped by a false reduction to molecule-talk.

However man arrived at this, this is how he is. Biological evolution is a useful concept in the molecule-talk. Evolutionists admit a 'jump' to psycho-social evolution (though language often slips uneasily). To be 'me' is to part company with animals and the 'lower creation'; thought, feeling, awareness, even conscience, make 'me' more complex, more wonderful, capable of things beyond any other earthly species, capable for good or ill – a creature of grief and glory but one who in recent times has been strangely prepared to trade both for the dull, mechanistic account of molecules and impulses.

# 5 Us

## No man is an island

John Donne's much-quoted words, 'All of mankind is part of me . . . never send to ask for whom the bell tolls; it tolls for thee', go some way to clearing up the 'man or Man' question. To be human is to be involved with other people, and not only with other people living at present, but with man as a species. Hence the Humanists' pride in Man, when they think of moon landings or triumphs over disease or drought, is justified. Hence, Christians would say, their own feeling of union with worshippers throughout the centuries – the sense of 'belonging' that they experience, for example, in an old country church – is a true mark of humanity. We share in the experiences of others and enter into even those of long ago, for in them we sense part of our own possibilities and dangers. Probably Jung's theories of psychological archetypes express a similar fact. For better or worse being human involves links with other people. There are occasional efforts to deny this, to live as though it were not true. Simon and Garfunkel's song 'I am a rock . . . ' expresses the anguished reaction to hurtful personal relationships:

> 'If I never loved I never would have cried . . .
> I touch no one and no one touches me.
> I am a rock, I am an island
>  And a rock feels no pain, and an island never cries.'

But such outbursts are a denial of humanity, a cutting off of part of being human.

This is a dramatic widening of sphere and will be broken down to two main areas to facilitate discussion. This present chapter which I have entitled 'Us' will deal with 'me' in relationships which can be described as personal, in small groups or with individuals. The next chapter which I have called 'Them' will cover the wider relationships within society, the ordering of large groups, nations, peoples and interests. I influence 'us' by the sort of person I am, my speech and inter-personal action. I influence 'them' in less direct ways – by the way I vote, by organizing pressure groups or lobbies, by writing or administration. The 'them' problems are often the 'us' problems writ large, but ironically they always seem more interesting and more tractable. It seems so much easier to prescribe solutions to political disturbance in Northern Ireland than to sort out the office squabbles over boy-friends, or the petty point-scoring of the dis-contented family. A lot of the Bible – and other religious writing – is about 'us' and 'them'. Humanists turn their main attention here, too, and provide much useful analysis and many programmes for reform and develop-ment.

## Us–talk

### 1. The language of relationships
The personal language we referred to earlier has lots of loose ends ready to latch on to experiences with other people. But it is, ultimately, a selfish language. It des-cribes how *I* feel, what *I* decide, *my* intellectual excite-ment at working out a correct solution to a problem or watching the sunset. The world is my oyster; it all exists for me (subject, of course, to the remarks that were made about the Christian view of God as Giver; but that will need fuller thought later).

When I am involved with other people, however, I find myself using a lot of words that don't have any true place in 'me-talk': words like love, hate, argue, betray, loyalty, duty. The word 'responsible' is a key word in considering the Humanist world-view. It was briefly mentioned in the last chapter and will be given a thorough airing in the next. For the moment, note that it comes powerfully into 'us-talk'. It is a colder word than 'concern' or 'I'm worried about Jim', and only a pale part (though a necessary part) of 'love'. In 'us-talk' love is very important so a little time may usefully be spent seeing what it is and what it is not.

## 2. 'Love', a key word

The Greeks had at least four words for it. They were lucky. English makes do with one poor overworked, misused word. 'Love' means different things to the pop-singer, preacher, sonnet-writer or Young Liberal. For many, it is tied to the sexual side of human nature, and always has some warm, sensual overtone – this is the *eros* of the Greeks, the desire to possess and be possessed, the complete devotion for which the world is well lost.

There is also friendship, the Greek *philia*, affection based upon common interests. Traditionally this has not involved any clear sexual component, but nowadays the knowing wink assures us there's no smoke without fire, and a tame psychologist is always at hand to tell us that all such personal involvement must have a sexual basis really. All agree that love is a powerful motivating force, and also that it is intuitive, if not 'blind'; it is usually seen standing against reason, calculation, even duty. Love overrides all. In fact, some of the pop-culture suggests strongly that 'love' is the only reality.

Humanists are therefore a little cagey about 'love' since their money is basically on reason. Their evolutionary motif also makes it hard for them to dissociate love from the physical. It lies down among the impulses, and you will usually find it discussed in chapters dealing with sexual morality, or adolescent development, though occasionally it gets the treatment it deserves as a deep inter-personal concern. Biological urge is, of course, inextricably woven into many experiences of love, especially adolescent ones, but that does not mean that love is to be reduced to molecule-talk. It is also closely linked with sincerity and responsibility, self-giving and duty, and so cannot long stay at the level of mere fun or casual diversion. Morton Hunt seems a little sorry about this:

' . . . modern love, being as important as it is and consisting ideally of a fusion of roles and values, cannot be genially and lightheartedly parcelled out. . . . Or at least not until society itself provides some new and yet-undiscovered mechanisms to embody the values now forced upon love, and to the needs it now satisfies. Conceivably some future social order may provide us, on a rational and orderly basis, with emotional reassurance and security, the satisfaction of our sexual drives, the fulfilment of our yearning for companionship and fellowship, and the yearly requirements of our social order for young. If so, love may become once again, as in the past, a frolic and an amusement, rather than an earnest and demanding business.'[1]

Dr James Hemming is not so anxious to avoid the demanding business. He sees clearly that the development of the whole person demands a break with childish egocentricity, and the endurance of suffering:

'Suffering is a mode of intense experience and is, therefore, formative. Indeed, there can be no intense experience without suffering. To strive is to suffer, for we shall often fail and fall short: to love is to suffer,

[1] Essay 'Love in a Humanist Frame' in J. Huxley (ed.), *The Humanist Frame*, p. 196.

because our concern for those we love will carry us into suffering. . . . '[2]

There may be an occasional look over the shoulder at the Christian commandment to love; a fear lest someone might suggest that Christians have already cornered the love market before Humanists got there. For whatever reason, Humanists often have a knock at the 'Love your neighbour' command. Karl Popper writes: 'Even the best Christian who really lives up to this commandment (there are not many, as is shown by the attitude of the average good Christian towards "materialists" and "atheists"), even he cannot feel equal love for all men.'[3]

H. J. Blackham devotes some space to it in writing of 'The Humanist Himself' and incidentally gives a useful insight into the Humanist understanding of inter-personal relationships:

'Love or friendship as more or less exclusive choice of persons with whom one is identified is in its nature special, not general. And I cannot love my neighbour in the sense of giving as much care and attention to his interests as to my own and those of my dependants and closest friends. I simply cannot love my neighbour as myself literally. In this sense it is a stupid requirement.

However, there are certain important and abiding ways in which I am identified with my neighbour although he is not a chosen friend. However I may dislike him or feel contempt for him, however unworthy of man his behaviour may be, he remains worthy of respect as a human being and a unique end in himself. He is autonomous, his own man, a source. Whatever the facts of his life, he has human possibilities. However often he belies them, better possi-

[2] J. Hemming, *Individual Morality* (Nelson, 1969), p. 144, and see the discussion on pp. 114–115.
[3] K. Popper, *The Open Society and its Enemies* (Routledge, 1943), chapter 24.

bilities are open to him, and it is in this sense that forgiveness is always due to him: whilst he lives the last word has not been said, and his future is not fully and finally judged by his past. These moral facts justify fellow-feeling and require a helping hand and imaginative treatment, and forbid censorious judgments, not to say humiliation that degrades or mocks his human dignity. I cannot love the unlovable nor admire what is not admirable, but I can indeed respect the human being in anyone and help him towards his better possibilities. Tolerance, tenderness, fellow-feeling of this kind is due from every man to every man.'[4]

Christians deserve most of what they get of this criticism. For all the talk about loving, there has been more often a sarcastic rather than a surprised tone in the cry, 'See how these Christians love one another!'

Some recent radical writing has gone to the extreme of stepping reason down in favour of love. The intuitive will give the right action where reason will blunder. In *Honest to God*, for instance, Dr J. A. T. Robinson tells us:

'Love alone, because, as it were, it has a built-in moral compass, enabling it to "home" intuitively upon the deepest needs of the other, can allow itself to be directed completely by the situation.'[5]

There is, as his paragraph heading put it, 'Nothing prescribed, except love'. In this he was popularizing the writings of the 'situation ethics' school of thought to whom 'love' becomes the only absolute. The criticism of this line of thought has fastened upon its inconclusiveness. If 'love is all' how am I to recognize it? Intuitions are notoriously difficult to judge. If 'love' means an unlimited concern for the good of others, what is 'good'? I

[4] H. J. Blackham, *Humanism*, p. 79.
[5] J. A. T. Robinson, *Honest to God* (SCM, 1963), p. 115.

must have some outside yardstick of what is good before 'love' can get going. To use an analogy from physics, love is like the voltage applied to a circuit which produces warmth or motion. But it shows itself useful only when the circuit is there for it to flow through.

The great commandment includes 'love . . . with all your mind'. Christians need to spell out much more carefully what this means. The New Testament word *agapē* seems to have been little used in classical Greek. Its New Testament use, not least in 1 Corinthians 13, shows it to be a term involving the whole person. It is certainly not limited to those feelings which may have a sexual expression or basis. It is the intelligent direction of the personality to the good of another, considering the circumstances of the relationship and what is appropriate to it. We may find it hard to realize how revolutionary the Christian idea was in the first-century world. *Agapē* was a (nearly) new word for a new idea. Aristotle agreed substantially with Mr Blackham (quoted above) that 'love' was an exclusive relation with those you liked. Plato said love is for the lovely. Epictetus did not rate it very highly. New Testament writers were introducing something new and revolutionary; and in spite of the sordid misuse of centuries, there is still something about 'love' that makes it one of the great words of human relationship.[6]

It is one of the great words in the new language, the us-talk.

### 3. Us-talk not reducible to me-talk

The whole of us-talk is under heavy fire. Just as me-talk is in danger of reduction to molecule-talk, so us-talk is in danger of going down a step to me-talk, or even, with the wilder behaviourists, to molecule-talk. These wilder reducers point out that all group relations have bio-

[6] See William Barclay, *Flesh and Spirit* (SCM, 1962), p. 63 for a careful discussion.

logical and social origins. The working group, the child-producing and child-rearing units, the fighting unit, all have their needs, impulses and pressures and so have evolved the appropriate reactions to ensure survival. This is just another example of 'nothing-buttery'. Humanists might accept the evolutionary origin but would insist that here is a 'jump' that has given rise to experience in its own right. They are prone to retreat to evolutionary explanations, however, when anyone mentions absolute standards of inter-personal behaviour, but their writing elsewhere shows they don't really intend to settle for observer descriptions only.

The reduction to me-talk is rather more subtle. It suggests that motives for actions are always selfish and that everything can therefore be described in terms of what I want. I don't need a word to describe relations with a friend, as I can express it all in the satisfaction I get, the sense of achievement, the boost to my ego, in having him around. He becomes a thing, just like any other part of nature. I still reign supreme. Everything serves me. Family relationships are easy meat for this reductionism. The drives for sexual satisfaction, food and security are strong and find an answer in marriage. 'Married love' is just a way the tender-minded dress up their selfishness, because they cannot accept themselves as selfish predators. And so the debunking spreads. All inter-personal relationships of service, care, sharing or concern are boiled down to desire for status, self-gratification, or something else in the me-talk vocabulary.

The assault on this devaluation is difficult. The devaluer can always postulate deeper and deeper levels of self-deception. The argument usually turns out to be circular, assuming the universal selfishness it sets out to prove. John, for example, has lived with himself all his life, knows his own self-deceptions and weaknesses to some extent. If he tells me that his care for someone is altruistically motivated, how am I to deny it? Have I, from the outside, any better access to his subconscious, self-deceiving desires than he has from the inside? But, says the devaluer, he *must* be getting something out of it or he wouldn't do it. Why? Because nobody does. Which is exactly what he was supposed to be proving!

## Human relationships

### 1. The family

The most important 'us' area is the family – an opportunity for personal relations we didn't choose. We choose our friends on the basis, among other things, of mutual interests. No-one chooses their parents. Parents don't choose their children, though they increasingly choose whether and when to have them. Some Humanists, deeply committed to man's control of everything, think parents should choose the children they have, for example by selecting the appropriate genes from a central gene-bank:

'What is needed is an application of that same sense of social responsibility that we already employ in the education, training and nourishing of the next generation to the provision for them, before procreation, of the best genetic equipment that is available. This means a replacement of our long-ingrained proprietary attitude that takes it for granted that the children one brings up should carry one's own genetic material. A deeper sense of fulfilment and at least as much affection, pride and feeling of identification in regard to the children one brings up will be evoked when one has chosen the germ-cells from which those children were derived with as much solicitude and as careful consideration and wise counselling as possible, from whatever available genetic sources one prefers or regards as most ideal. As it becomes realized that techniques, involving germ-cell banks and controlled implantation, are at hand for achieving this end . . . the new more of having children of choice rather than of "fate" will gradually become more prevalent.'[7]

It is true that this is a very *avant-garde* Humanist view, but it is in line with the 'we-know-best' psycho-social evolutionary philosophy. It is also this sort of comment that gets the attention.

The family has been under heavy criticism from the beginning. Man is the only species that requires so long for offspring to become independent and hence some child-rearing system has to be devised. Plato wanted children raised communally by the state to avoid the petty interests of family groupings, and he has had advocates since then. Recent sociology doesn't always help him.[8] It seems that 'mother substitutes' don't do the same job in nurture and security, and local authorities are much less ready to sever the child's relationships with his mother than they were. Reports on the Israeli kibbutzim suggest that children so raised find it difficult to make truly personal relationships or to make personal, as opposed to group, decisions. Too little is known of the Chinese commune system to say whether it is a successful substitute for the family.

Critics of the family – especially younger critics – often see it as a bastion against social change. Parents pass on their values slowly to their children and make the educators' task much more difficult. Social change is slowed down. It is true that parents often *are* selfish, regarding their children as extensions of themselves. Sometimes they are violent. Present family structure tends to perpetuate social class and literacy distinctions. There are plenty of autobiographies and novels to show how things can go wrong in the family. It is much harder to write a convincing novel of the normal, undramatic, successful family life.

[7] H. J. Miller in *The Humanist Frame*, p. 412.
[8] John Bowlby, *Child Care and the Growth of Love* (Penguin, 1957).

64

Christians have been thinking and writing about family relationships for a long time – and they took over from the Hebrews who had been at it as long and who still represent probably the most family-conscious of all people. Christian practice has not matched the fine words and good intentions, though very many Christian families fare much better than their critics allow. They start with a definite 'place to stand'. Marriage is ordained of God, with purposes that include, as the Book of Common Prayer affirms, the bringing up of children in the fear and nurture of the Lord and also, for the mutual society, help and comfort that each may have of the other. Christians therefore start with a manufacturer's blueprint. How well they follow it is another story.

Humanists lean to scientific explanations and reasons and are influenced by their evolutionary motif of development to ever better things. For them there is no manufacturer, no blueprint, no absolute, so they have an open field in which to write widely, and sometimes wildly.

An example of radical treatment was Edmund Leach's Reith Lectures of 1967[9] from which the following extracts are taken:

'Family values have become increasingly focused on private status rather than public good . . . perhaps it is family life itself that needs to be changed rather than the parents. Psychologists, doctors, schoolmasters, and clergymen put over so much soppy propaganda about the virtue of a united family life that most of you probably have the idea that "the family", in our English sense, is a universal institution, the very foundation of organized society. This isn't so. Human beings at one time or another have managed to invent all sorts of different styles of domestic living and we shall have to invent still more in the future.

. . . Today the domestic household is isolated. The

[9] Published as *A Runaway World* (BBC, 1968).

family looks inward upon itself; there is an intensification of emotional stress between husband and wife and parents and children. The strain is greater than most of us can bear. Far from being the basis of a good society, the family, with its narrow privacy and tawdry secrets, is the source of all our discontents. (A footnote to the published version expresses surprise at "public animosity provoked by this very ordinary remark. The contemporary English monogamous, neo-local, nuclear family with its matrifocal emphasis is historically an unusual form of domestic grouping. Although it gives a relatively high status to the wife-mother it presupposes that woman's natural role is that of cook-housekeeper-nursemaid.")

. . . It is not at all obvious what the change should be . . . kin groups can only function effectively if most of the members are clustered together in one place and this requirement conflicts with one of the prime dogmas of capitalist free enterprise: the freedom to move around and sell your labour in the best market.

. . . I don't know the answer . . . Our present society is emotionally very uncomfortable. The parents and children huddled together in their loneliness take too much out of each other. The parents fight; the children rebel. Children need to grow up in larger, more relaxed domestic groups centred on the community rather than in mother's kitchen; something like an Israeli kibbutz or a Chinese commune.'[1]

This is colourful stuff, lapped up by the press – especially the Christian press who rise to the bait and denounce Humanism as the prime underminer of moral standards and family life.[2] (There are plenty of other agencies they could turn their fire on, such as the hedonism of pop-culture and the materialistic criteria peddled by the

[1] *Op. cit.*, pp. 43ff.
[2] *E.g.* in *The Christian* of 17 August 1968, under the large headline 'Humanist view of marriage': 'Marriage has been rejected as a

glossy magazines.) Humanists are avowed individual-ists and none would think of curbing Leach's diatribe. But his is not the typical Humanist voice. James Hemming, for example, says quite the opposite:

> 'The need of society, in view of our present knowledge, is to promote quality in marriage. . . . Five patterns of bonds may be distinguished in the human family: the bond of the child to the mother . . . of the mother to the child . . . of the parents together . . . between father and children . . . and the bond between the young ones. A further bond, the bond between children in the family and other children – the very important social bond – itself largely arises from the inner security and self-confidence created by the inter-familial bonds. The loving and lively family nest is the basis of future mental and moral health within society.'[3]

It is true that the survey of 1964 (see note 3, p. 8) showed 5% of members of the Humanist Association as separated or divorced (thirty times the national average), but the majority of Humanists live stably and securely married, and struggle to bring up children fairly and freely. The writing of such people is very valuable, focusing attention on the personal relationships rather than the social structure. Like convinced Christians, convinced Humanists find themselves a minority, often cherishing values they feel are attacked – Christians by secular society, Humanists by what they see as a religious establishment represented by school assembly and RE. And so the bookish among them express themselves maturely and sincerely. The non-bookish probably feel similar tensions and anxieties and hopes, but do not write about it; they just get on with the business of living

sacred or indispensable part of society in a statement received at the annual conference of the British Humanist Association in Loughborough. . . . '
[3] James Hemming, *Individual Morality*, p. 220.

and bringing up the kids decently. Here is an area where informal meeting of parents, Christian and Humanist, would be welcome. The embattled ideologies could recede before shared experience of actual interest, care and love for children. Each has a lot to learn from the other. The following extract from Virginia Flemming's *Humanist Parents and Teachers*, for example, would be common ground for a start:

'The task which falls upon parents and others of cherishing children so that each child grows up free from resentful anxiety, and so that the first stirrings of fellow feeling in each are reinforced by a social life guided by loving fairness, is perhaps too great for frail humanity. It would be if imperfection and failure were really fatal. But if the underlying will and feeling are sound, even recurrent loss of temper and injustices are not fatal if they are acknowledged as failures, for the guiding principles are thereby acknowledged too. Children under six have a genius for loving forgiveness if they are given half a chance, and a genius for feeling deeper intentions. Incidentally they learn something of the true nature of the human attempt to live well through the admitted failures of their mother.'[4]

It is in the transmission of their ideology that Humanists find most difficulty. Anxious to be true to their ideal of 'openness' and to let the children develop for themselves, they yet feel they have much to offer, although mildly embarrassed at the 'negativeness' of their position. Virginia Flemming, in the pamphlet just quoted, warns her fellow-Humanist parents against

'a loss of nerve through allowing themselves to feel that their outlook is merely negative because they are

[4] Virginia Flemming, *Humanist Parents and Teachers* (Ethical Union, 2nd ed., 1957), p. 4.

68

inarticulate about their deepest convictions and have nothing to put forward corresponding to the Christian religion. This is easier said than done, for children of the most articulate and dedicated humanists do tend to think of their parents as simply *not* believing and not going to church.'[5]

Christians should have some sympathy as they face the task of bringing children up 'in the nurture and admonition of the Lord' in a non-Christian society, at the same time trying to respect the child's freedom. In an interesting pamphlet *Religion and Your Child*, Humanist parents write frankly and sympathetically of their children in a way that might surprise Christians who read only the wilder stuff in the popular press.

' . . . It certainly came as a bit of a shock when the eldest lad at the age of sixteen declared his wish to be baptised. We regret he does not see things as we do. But we felt that for a lad of that age to present himself for a ceremony usually undergone by babies represented a certain moral integrity and courage, and we were glad to accept his invitation to go along with him on that occasion.'[6]

Some survive the religious pressures:

'We are a closely-knit family and I am happy to say that my elder son, who is now adolescent, has become the youth I hoped for – clean-living and clear-thinking . . . The younger boy is following in his brother's footsteps and I have no fears now. Our motto is "Be true to yourself".'[7]

[5] *Op. cit.*, p. 7.
[6] C. Bibby in *Religion and your Child* (RPA, 1959), p. 12.
[7] Beatrice Baikie in *op. cit.*, p. 34.

Some don't, and parents wonder:

> 'We now think that we made a mistake in not finding out more about the teaching of these organizations at an earlier stage, and endeavouring to combat their influence. We thought our son would eventually out-grow such beliefs. . . . On the other hand, participation in these organizations has given him much more confidence in dealing with situations and with people.'[8]

Again, because of their functional approach and emphasis, Humanists seem to write more about the family as a child-rearing institution than about relations between parents – 'the mutual society that each should have of the other'. It is, of course, the bookish who express themselves, and they are most likely to have a wide range of shared interests and a good cultural background. They do not regard it *de fide* as a lifelong relationship: it must justify itself continually by reference to the needs of the partners. James Hemming writes that 'the ideal will continue to be a partnership so rich in potential that exploring the mutual experience of one another is in itself deeply satisfying – strong loves need no paramours'. Nevertheless he sees the future when 'a much wider range of possibilities will be accepted in society. Some couples may live together without ever marrying; some will plunge into marriage at first love and risk the consequences; some will marry after a period of maturing personally and physically in the search for the right marriage partner'.[9]

Nor is there, in Humanist writing, a lot of reference to family through the eyes of the teenage children – except to speak of emancipation from religiously intolerant parents, and the occasional more sensitive autobiography. Once the home has done its child-rearing stuff,

[8] 'R.T.' in *op. cit.*, pp. 22f.
[9] James Hemming, *Individual Morality*, pp. 223, 225.

of course there is no absolute reason why relationship should be more than that of good friends, though many Humanists show care and devotion of a high order to aged, infirm parents.

## 2. Marriage

What does family relationship do to personal development? Is it limiting? or deepening? Marriage is the undertaking of a responsibility. Christians see this as promises made in God's presence. Humanists have no such sanction and refer to sociological implications, as for example Mrs M. B. Simms in a BBC interview:

> 'Marriages which produce children, but don't last very long, are obviously, from a social point of view, very undesirable; clearly, if you wish to have children then you must try to think of marriage as a permanent state.' (A footnote to the published edition adds, 'though not an indissoluble one, in the religious sense'.)[1]

Living closely together makes people conscious of their own (and others') shortcomings and strengths. New causes of both respect and irritation arise. If it has to endure suffering or economic pressure, the family brings out the worst or the best in the individuals involved. Dr Leach (quoted above) thinks this is making demands greater than the members can bear. He also complains about the 'loneliness' of the members of the family, 'huddled together'. Yet this is precisely a strength; a place where one is known and accepted in the middle of an anonymous and increasingly mobile society. In the family is opportunity for the development of trust, a relationship of open sincerity, where one need not fear to know and to be known. It is here that infant egocentricity gets its first check, and here, too, that adult selfishness meets its greatest challenge.

[1] Mrs M. B. Simms in *An Inquiry into Humanism* (BBC, 1966), p. 14.

In talking about being human, it is important to emphasize that these relationships are the strong meat of humanity, what married life is about. It is the trust, concern, self-giving, acceptance, admiration, open criticism, that are valuable, however expressed. The current image, helped on by the mass media, is of the importance of sexual expression. The presence on a recent young people's house-party of a married couple, both in wheel-chairs, the girl paralysed from the waist down, gave many of us valuable pause to think. Some were surprised, in wondering what marriage meant in those circumstances, to find how largely sexual expression had dominated their own thinking. Humanists, of course, have accused Christians of regarding sex as an unfortunate necessity – and they have no difficulty in dredging up quotes from Jerome and elsewhere, some of them quite recent. But at the moment it would be more helpful if they could concentrate on the substance of marriage, the relationship and confidence which is expressed in sexual relation. So much mass media and paperback/magazinery give the impression that good sexual technique is the one essential to successful marriage. But if you have nothing to say, the most cultured Oxford accent isn't much good to you. When you do have something to say, it is worth thinking how to say it well.

## 3. Friendship

The other major area of 'us-talk' is in friendship, whether the club, institute, chat over the gate, or the more diverse friendships of youth. Young people have – or seem to have – rather more time than their elders for this activity. They also have a lot of money to spend on leisure so a market in this has quickly arisen. But going places together or spending money together isn't necessarily a very personal activity. Team games are less in vogue than formerly, though small group activities such as seeing Europe or ventures that require skill of some kind are booming. The chief influence these have on character-forming are the opportunities they give for seeing other people in action, understanding how they think and what they take as important, and the incentives they provide for effort. 'As iron sharpens iron, so a man sharpens the countenance of his friend.' The principal areas of development in the 15–25 age range are in attitudes to authority, especially parents, and in attitudes to the opposite sex.

Humanists root for the Open Society, so authority patterns have to be minimal. They thus find themselves on the side of the young. Rigid structures in society are liable to be condemned; it is through change that improvement comes, so the urges of the young to change everything are welcome. It has been interesting to note recently, however, in connection with student disturbance, that *Humanist* has carried some fairly strong stuff against the 'minority' who are going beyond rational criticism and aiming to destroy the existing system. This is not paradoxical, since the Humanist emphasis is equally on the Open Society and the rational society. Criticism is valuable if it is rationally motivated. Change what you like as long as you can put forward arguments for it. But 'Destroy because I find it frustrating' is not acceptable – not because it is 'wrong' in any absolute sense, but because it cannot help forward man's rational improvement of his condition. Humanists welcome discussion, argument, controversy among the young. This will develop powers of thought, expression, and clear away the cobwebs of tradition and inherited patterns of behaviour. Let people think and act for themselves.

Christians might show a little more enthusiasm for this approach themselves, even if they doubt that youth is any less likely to go wrong than any other age group. They might certainly take note of the highly developed social awareness of today's young people. This may, far back, have come from a Christian stable, though the young people often find churches complacent and deaf to their ideals. It is doubtful whether a Humanist ground can support the idealism. It would be tragic if it petered out in 'If you can't beat them, join them', and at thirty they are all found treading the materialist road to 'success'.

Humanists are also against anything they see as irrational or prejudiced limitations on sexual expression. They are sure Christians are against anyone enjoying sex, and their anthropological, evolutionary approach makes them think sex isn't all that special among the impulses, and certainly not 'sacred' as Christians might suggest. They do stand for personal relationship as the criterion and it is unfair to put them alongside the modern hedonist whose motto is 'If you like it, have it'. Promiscuity is as contemptible to most Humanists as to Christians, but they would consider that marriage is a civil contract and that sexual relations express personal relations quite separately from the contractual side of marriage. The depth and integrity of the relation is what matters. Experiment, they would say, is no bad thing either, provided it is not exploitation. In all this they assume no children will be produced. This (for them) is the unpardonable sin, to produce an unwanted child. They are in the forefront of pressure for sex education, greater availability of contraceptives and contraceptive advice, abortion when things have gone wrong. Whatever the result of their propaganda, it would be wrong to charge them with wanting sexual anarchy. They see themselves as trying to break down centuries of sexual inhibition and slavery.

Many people, Christian or Humanist, may feel that the pressure of advertising, TV, cinema, *etc.* makes it increasingly difficult for young people to have normal friendships, developing and maturing themselves as they share interests with others. They must always have the unpleasant suspicion that they are desired as a possible sex-object, not as a personal friend; or else they experience the alarm of wondering if they can be 'normal' when so much heterosexual friendship around them has sexual expression.

Some of the 'new morality' pronouncements by churchmen have not helped. They are probably right to show that all that goes on in marriage is not necessarily good, nor the expression of deep love. But what has come across to the general public is that, if sexual intercourse between unmarried, or even un-engaged, young people is the expression of a deep love, then it's all right. The multiplying of cases – many invented by ingenious film-script writers – where traditional sexual codes have brought sorrow, or their breach has brought some release, does not help. The situation ethics merchants seem to suggest that hard cases make law bad.

For themselves, Christians are bound by the words of Jesus and his apostles. He spoke of fornication as an evil thing which defiles the man,[2] not a therapeutic blessing for his neuroses. While this is binding upon those who profess to follow him, and while we may well think that the designer knows what is best for the machine, Christians may nevertheless cut little ice by quoting this in general discussion. If it is 'best for the machine' then some hint of this can probably be discovered by looking at the machine. Hence Christian apologetic in the field of sexual ethics and the relationships of young people will best be done from a sociological and personal basis,[3] with the occasional plain statement and elucidation of the Christian view.[4] Christians need to put much more emphasis on the development of the person and the nature of relationships than has happened in the past. What does this type of liaison do to the people involved? Does it really help the growth of dignity, self-respect and respect for the other? What does it do to the status of

[2] Mark 7: 20–23.
[3] *E.g.* E. M. Duvall, *Why wait till marriage?* (Hodder and Stoughton, 1966).
[4] *E.g.* V. A. Demant, *An Exposition of Christian Sex Ethics* (Hodder and Stoughton, 1963).

marriage quite apart from any legal considerations of responsibility? As Lord Devlin has commented, monogamy has been built into our way of living. It got there because it was Christian. It stays there because the house would fall down if it were pulled out. Opponents have got to convince us they have alternative means of keeping the house up.

## 4. At work

The other principal 'us' area open to many people is in the field of work. For some this may seem a mockery; they clock in at 7.59 and perform the same operation on the same machine in the same noise until 10.30 when tea break comes. But even tea break brings some powerful us-ness. Some jobs require less noise, if equally little concentration, and here the whole work time is often spent in chatter, gossip, and occasional pearls of wisdom. Sometimes trivial, crude, bawdy or even malicious, yet sometimes full of earthy wisdom, such groups play their part in developing personality. Particularly for the less able or those doing the routine jobs, there is often an accepting atmosphere. One is allowed to be oneself, not just part of the productive process. Whatever the attitude of management – and even they may unbend a little – the small work-group may have its part in being human, with its 'us-talk' of sympathy, acceptance, responsibility, codes of judgment, which occasionally blossom out into mutual help outside the place of work. If the work is more demanding, and the group remains small, there arise other inter-personal relationships. There is the reliance upon the special skills of each member of the group, the growing experience that the group thrives only when these skills are cheerfully contributed – if George is in a bad temper today, it may be harder to get him to do his bit of plumbing so that we can get on with the carpentry.

This is not to say that all work-groups are idyllic settings where humanity flourishes and noble thoughts are shared! Of course there is just the same opportunity for George to develop the most cussed temper, and Bert to slack unconscionably. But this, too, is part of humanity. Relationships between persons can be good or bad – the tragedy of some mass-production systems is that personal relations may be non-existent in a purely functional coming and going of 'human' operatives.

Again, a lot of thought is overdue about the nature of this relationship between workers. What are the limits and nature of responsibility? How may each 'consider the other for his own good'? What causes of friction are there, and how may they be reduced? What can be done *within the system* to ease the tensions? For example, as Symanowski[5] points out, modern industry and shift work, even if it allows small relatively stable work-groups, means that a man has more real comity of interest with workmates, and spends far longer with them than with his wife and children. Efforts to change the system, by Humanist or Christian, are worth serious attention, but meanwhile thousands of people could do with sympathetic attention to their relationships in their present situations. There is some evidence that Christians are waking up to their responsibilities here, though somewhat tardily and still at the bookish level. Humanists are well aware of the larger problem of anonymity and pointlessness in large work units – and James Hemming, for example, in his Conway lecture[6] argues for 'participation' at all levels. But at the small group level, when one considers the contribution to personality of the daily round and the relationship between 'me and my mates', there is very little literature. At the workshop level there probably doesn't need to be a lot of literature, because the workers here are not bookish. But there does need to be a lot more understanding, pastoral care and

[5] Horst Symanowski, *The Christian Witness in an Industrial Society* (Collins, 1966), chapter 8.
[6] James Hemming, *The Alternative Society* (51st Conway Memorial Lecture; South Place Ethical Society, 1969).

support, and a sustained effort – perhaps at mass media level – to redeem daily work from its present status as a necessary evil and probably a waste of time anyway.

**Relationship between 'us', 'me' and 'nature'**

The simple me–nature tension of the last chapter now becomes a three-cornered contest. It needs a triangle to show it.

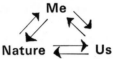

When we introduce 'them' it will become still more complicated, but for the moment 'us' introduces enough complications to be going on with.

The tension between 'me' and 'us' is the meat of most literature. It is not just selfishness, my determining to have my own way against some outsider. It is the tension between what I want for myself and an 'us' of which I form part. The man who flies off the handle at his kids knows that in damaging them he hurts what is dear to himself. In saner moments he deplores his own lack of consideration to his wife or his disloyalty to his mates. He may take refuge in his 'rights'; children may cut fine poses about 'possessive' parents. But these do not satisfy most people most of the time. They are, rather, defence mechanisms to protect a narrow self-interest and put off admission of it. But apology, however grudging or crude, is a recurring feature of all these relationships – a demonstration, if one were needed, that the responsibility and loyalty involved are 'written in their hearts', that love and duty are irreducible words of us-talk that we cannot live without.

The 'us', of course, exerts powerful influence on 'me'. At worst it may be over-protective, stopping me developing my own personality fully. This may not happen as often as children think, but it does happen and few things are more sadly observed by schoolmasters than parents who try to re-live their lives in clever children. But there is also support, encouragement, healthy criticism.

What does nature do in this threesome? I may have learned to come to terms with the limitations it imposes upon me, but can 'we' come to similar terms? The wife who insists on pushing her husband to keep up with the Joneses is probably as little help as the friend whose embarrassment makes him unable to accept a handicapped person readily. Two are stronger than one, and the larger group is more powerful still. Whatever the quality of personal relations within them, the kibbutzim have worked wonders agriculturally, and a further reference to the monks in their fields and woodlands is not amiss. A marked feature of recent scientific, and especially medical, research has been its group character. Small teams of highly skilled, closely dependent scientists have made some impressive inroads on disease and famine.

At the same time, control over nature has posed some new, as well as some very old, problems. At the family level, more effective contraception has made possible new decisions about the number and spacing of children. The separation of the procreative and inter-spouse expressive features of sexual intercourse is another two-edged sword man's conquest of nature has given. It may permit the freer expression and deeper growth of tenderness and love, unhindered by fear of unwanted pregnancy; or it may provide another aid to selfish indulgence. It certainly makes possible the conscious choice between a baby boy or girl and baby car. Between the unmarried young, too, this control over nature poses fresh areas of decision. Prudential considerations of possible pregnancy no longer weigh heavily with the girls (it is doubtful if they ever did weigh very heavily with the boys), and an apologetic which pleads for chastity on the grounds of the hardships awaiting the illegitimate child is now largely misplaced. At most it will only make people more 'careful'. This will be an advantage if it raises the whole question of relationship, its nature and quality, and focuses attention on the young lovers themselves and not only on the possible outcome.

Control over nature raises problems at the other end with life extended by twenty years or more. Humanists – and some Christians – here find the most likely solution in euthanasia. The difficulties are admitted, principally those that arise from human selfishness. But, they argue, only in this way can dignity be maintained. The geriatric wards, and the increasing number of old folk's homes certainly pose the problems, personal as well as sociological. Can you be human when you get old? What are the proper personal relationships when 'us' includes the aged? Whatever sociologists say, the problem is more personal than sociological. The aged are no great contributors to population explosions. The world will be strangled with *young* people long before the old and infirm cripple its resources.

## Another step to humanness

As these nature-me-us tensions mount it is no wonder some people try to break them by drastic reductionist techniques; no wonder people try to explain away 'responsibility' or 'love'; no wonder the temptation to dismiss all as molecule-talk becomes so strong. But to be human must involve at least all this. It may be a demanding and tense business, but in fact it is often a rewarding and enjoyable business and the 'us' makes for a great deal of the enjoyment.

# 6 Them

## The separated world outside

Within his home Mr Smith may be 'Jack' or 'Dad', and everybody is 'you' to everybody else: why don't *you* turn that record-player down? But as soon as he gets outside he is a road-user, owner of vehicle XYZ 123D, bank account number 1234560, family allowance book no. XB2345, and so on. There will still be the friend- or work-group where he is Jack, but otherwise he will be Mr Smith or 'Smith'. The bank computer will tell him his balance, and has been told to print out J. B. Smith, 24 Park Grove, Hudderstown when 1234560 comes up.

His own language will now show a difference. Why don't *they* mend the traffic lights, alter the one-way system, or reduce the tax on petrol? It is, in large measure, another world. Whatever care, irritation, acceptance, rejection happens at home, in this other world there is little personal touch – except in the advertising slogans. If there is *no* point of contact between the two worlds, then it is indeed a *separated* world, and for some young people especially, as the lyric has it, 'in the separated world outside, the heart of true living dies'. We are back at the questions of significance and replaceability that we mentioned earlier. But before we return to them, the language warrants a preliminary look at it again.

## What sort of language is this?

What is the difference between 'us' and 'them'? We are people; are 'they'? Probably, but in a rather abstract, disembodied way. When Mrs Smith comes back from her part-time job as typist at Mammoth Markets Ltd, she tells Jack, 'They're moving the wholesale side to Newcastle next month, so Joe says.' Joe is, within the personal language, one of the work-group with a personality of his own. 'They' are presumably the directors, or managers, but they have no personality, no relationship with Mrs Smith. She and her office-mates might write a protest or send a representative, but it would be to some nebulous 'them'. Mr Smith feels the same about the rates demand. He may be one of the minority who voted in the last local elections, but still the city fathers are 'they'. It's probably not their fault anyway that the rates are up, but the fault of – well, the result of – administrative decisions taken by a score of officials at the town hall. The civic machinery grinds on and 'they' have only limited power over it.

People have been blaming 'them' for centuries – and occasionally commending them. Recently a more sophisticated language has been available. In learned circles we no longer refer to 'them' but to 'society'. The 'commonwealth' or 'citizenry' have long been acceptable words among political writers. 'Society' is a more recent entrant, and is now very widely used. It has smuggled in quasi-personal uses (as 'nature' and 'evolution' have), so that people talk about 'society' doing this or that, and we are invited to consider the permissive, affluent or post-Christian society. It is an elusive concept. At one end I am told that society is made up of people, and therefore it is really warmly personal. At the other end I see social laws being put forward and every facet of society being examined by sociologists, and it all becomes coldly mechanistic. People can be either obstinate or martyrs in their resistance of society.

The most pressing problem comes when we try to combine us-talk with 'them' or society. Can we have a 'responsible' society, a loving society, a just society, a selfish society? What would all these mean? Can society *care*? Can it be blamed or praised?

It seems doubtful whether we need a fourth, separate area of language. If we talk about statistical observation of the behaviour of large numbers of people, we are really in the area of molecule-talk. This is how things happen. The social sciences can mark out several areas in which they can be as rigorous and accurate in their descriptions as chemists or physicists. The interaction of this with 'freedom' has already been looked at. No-one need get worked up about it. Social scientists are not going to reduce them to machines any more than bio-chemists are. But taking this sort of language out of 'them-talk' will put it in its right place and stop people getting the wrong idea about it. It will still leave a lot of things to say, and these will be seen to involve the same sort of words as 'us-talk' – not all the same words, but a selection of them. For example, 'responsibility' and 'duty' become key words. 'Justice' becomes an important word. It is doubtful whether 'love' features much in talk about society. In an institutional setting, the proper expression of love is justice. Similarly 'anger' at society will be something different from anger in a smaller group.

Two dangers appear to threaten. First, the ever-present reductionist will tell us that this is all a matter of sociological laws, development, pressures, *etc.*, and rob us of any objective responsibility or personal participation. Second, we may be emotionally dragged into responses which, though appropriate in the small group, are inappropriate in society at large. I doubt if I can love mankind, but I am called upon to love my neighbour – anyone who comes in my path to whom I may give personal support. The Oxfam and Christian Aid advertisements would make an interesting study here. Perhaps they have already settled that, for many people, the response is going to be a contribution as impersonal as the advertisement! At the national level, Oxfam does not campaign along these lines of personal care, but along the lines of justice and responsibility – what the state *ought* to do.

Humanists are really on their own chosen wicket in this field of society. This is where the bulk of their effort lies, and where the bulk of their writing and analysis has been done. From this they gain most of their popular image as outspoken protagonists of freedom. They have a social interest and concern that shames many Christians and it seems almost churlish to adopt a critical approach to their activities. Yet the criticism is not so much of their plans as of their foundations. They object, not unnaturally, to being called 'the cut flowers of a Christian culture',[1] but they have been less than successful in making their own presuppositions clear. Again it seems to come down to the fact that it is what they deny, not what they affirm, that separates them from Christians. Christians may rejoice – and might well rejoice a bit more – at the social achievements of the Humanists; but they may still say that their involvement and concern is a commitment, an act of faith as great in its way as Christian belief. Hence in moral and social education, Humanists are going to find themselves hard put to it to keep up the image of a rational, scientific basis. This is seen most clearly in matters of language. Hence we must examine a few key words.

## What is 'responsibility'?

It has already been hinted that 'responsibility' is a key

---

[1] H. J. Blackham (*Objections to Humanism*) is modest: 'The charge of "living on Christian capital" is not to be lightly dismissed solely because of the irritation it arouses.' But see, *e.g.*, Enid Rob (*Humanist*, December 1966) and Margaret Knight (*Humanist Outlook*, pp. 47 ff.) for angry retorts that 'anything that is worthwhile about religion is simply Humanism'.

word in relationships – both in a man's relations to his friends, and now in the wider area of society. Responsibility is clearly connected with 'response'. In Pavlovian psychology there are explanations of behaviour in terms of stimulus-response mechanisms, but this is a narrowing of meaning and not what Humanists want to say by 'responsibility'. It would cut out all praise and blame, all striving or meaning, and reduce everything to molecule-talk again. To be useful in discussion of social issues 'responsible' must mean 'answerable for one's choices'. H. J. Blackham defines Humanism as the making of two assumptions – 'of responsibility for one's own life and for the life of mankind'.[2] He recognizes that these are 'personal decisions' and devotes some space to justifying them, and admits that

'The notion of responsibility gives some difficulty. Strictly one is responsible to someone for something. If not responsible to God, to whom is man responsible? Who will make him accountable if there is not a last day? All the same, there is a recognizable sense in which responsibility may be real without meaning accountability to another to whom one is answerable. One speaks of "making oneself responsible for", and this is not to be given responsibility by another to whom one is accountable, but to take it upon oneself and thus to make oneself answerable to oneself. That this may be a real and solemn undertaking cannot seriously be doubted. Sanctions which responsibility always involves apply in this case also, for there is no more painful condition than to be self-condemned.'[3]

This is a serious attempt to deal with a real difficulty. It does not attempt to slide out in mechanistic ways, nor to reduce the feeling of responsibility to group standards or survival value or other such devaluations as occur all too often. But what does Mr Blackham actually tell us?

[2] H. J. Blackham, *Humanism*, p. 13.    [3] *Op. cit.*, pp. 14f.

How does one 'make oneself answerable to oneself'? Is there a higher self and a lower self? Is there a future self and past self? Or an ideal self and a self liable to slip? The Christian tends to get involved in trouble with the word 'self' – for example in talk of 'denying himself' (which Blackham won't have at any price),[4] or Paul's description of his inner conflict – but the tension there is between a new life of the Holy Spirit and the less-than-perfect ordinary human life in which we still have part. Mr Blackham, however, would not wish to postulate such an *alter ego*. Who, then, is the 'self' to whom I am asked to make myself responsible? And who does the 'making'? Is there a third 'self' who puts the lesser under the greater? Again, talking of 'sanctions', what is meant by 'self-condemned'? By what code is the man driven to self-condemnation? At the very least he stands under an 'ought', that he 'ought' to fulfil what he promises. But why should he, especially if it is to his disadvantage?

The idea is very imperfectly defined, and so it is not surprising that 'response' in Humanist literature is a very uncertain word. For example, 'one must be bound to the world by some bonds of love or respond to it with some excitement or enthusiasm before Humanism can help one. Humanism is not a substitute for this response, and is helpless without it. This mixed personal response to the world of hope and fear, love and hate, is the raw material to which Humanism gives definite shape and which again is finished off by the person for himself.[5] Here 'respond' is simply 'inter-action' and cannot carry any overtones of 'feeling responsible for'. And 'excitement' and 'enthusiasm' are neutral words: I may have little excitement or enthusiasm for doing my duty, yet my sense of responsibility may drive me to it. X may have great excitement and enthusiasm for quite the opposite; how am I to tell him his 'spontaneous response' should be modified?

[4] See *Humanism*, p. 77.   [5] *Op. cit.*, p. 18.

This brings into view the second difficulty Humanists have in getting off the ground. They want not only to confess their own 'personal decision' to assume responsibility, but want everyone else to act responsibly. Now they are quite entitled to ask and exhort other people to do so, but then they must shed the rational, scientific mantle, and adopt the role of preacher pleading for responsive faith. Because there is no evident logical connection between 'I make myself responsible for these people' and 'You must make yourself responsible for these people'. If there is any overarching principle of responsibility, if there is a God to whom we are responsible, then it is not a matter of exhorting people to accept responsibility, but to *recognize* that they *are* responsible and act accordingly. Much Humanist writing proceeds on the assumption that people are responsible – the word 'ought' comes in very often – but yet they shy off any clear statement of how this can be, and persist in saying there are 'no absolutes'. They can't have it both ways.

## The evolutionary ethics approach

Humanists often derive the word 'morality' from *mores*, and point out, quite rightly, that the *mores* is the body of customs, standards, behaviour of a society. This is what the people actually do. It may be possible to give social explanations of how these standards came to be accepted, or how these patterns of behaviour arose. Yet this is not using the word 'moral' in the same sense as when we use it to praise or blame people. We are then talking, not about what they *do* do, but about what they *ought* to do. In Humanist literature this confusion goes very deep, and there are frequent references to 'social, that is, moral values', 'anti-social and basically immoral', 'morals are created by society', 'values are entirely natural products'. Yet on other pages they describe apartheid, or Nazi genocide, or Communist imprisonments as immoral. But these are certainly things South Africans or Nazis or

Communists *do* do: it is part of their *mores*. So 'moral' will have to mean more than 'how a group *do* act'; the 'ought-ness' is built in somewhere into the use of the word.

How then, in the words of Jacques,[6] are we 'to account for our fundamental moral convictions'? The Christian traces it, as Paul expresses it in Romans, to the fact that 'what the law requires is written on their hearts'.[7] Whether rooted in man's rationality alone, or more widely, man's moral awareness is real, demanding, and understood as a demand from outside him which he did not invent and cannot escape. The non-bookish man at the bench does not give a lot of thought to it, but is convinced he is not alone is his moral convictions – 'You know as well as I do that you ought to' is his unsophisticated comment. Humanists are loath to accept any objective point of reference. 'No absolutes' is their watchword, though in practice it tends to get watered down to 'no absolutes, but you *must* respect the views of others'. Yet they do not wish to be relativists, allowing any code to be equally valid with any other. Karl Popper, in his essay in *Humanist Outlook*, expressly sets his face against relativism:

> 'This is not a concession to relativism. In fact, the very idea of error presupposes the idea of truth. Admitting that the other man may be right and that I may be wrong obviously does not and cannot mean that each man's personal point of view is equally true or equally tenable and that, as the relativists say, everybody is right within his own frame of reference, though he may be wrong within that of somebody else.'[8]

Professor Morris Ginsberg takes moral judgments to be 'genuine judgments in the sense that they are capable of

[6] J. H. Jacques, *The Right and the Wrong* (SPCK, 1965).
[7] Romans 2: 15.
[8] Karl Popper, 'Emancipation through Knowledge' in *The Humanist Outlook*, p. 295.

being true or false, and . . . like other judgments, they are subject to rational tests, such as consistency and coherence'.[9] And the general body of their writing on social issues has a broadly objective ring – this *ought* to be done, that *must* be remedied, the law is unjust, censorship is too rigid – except when they wish to argue for more liberal laws in certain directions, and then sexual standards are said to be the individual's own business (as long as he doesn't hurt someone else) or parental authority or school discipline is decried (as long as no-one is hurt).

When it comes to 'accounting for our fundamental moral convictions' they seem always to slip into evolutionary explanations, at peril of reducing everything to molecule-talk once again. 'After all, values are phenomena, and therefore capable of being investigated by the methods of science', says Julian Huxley.[1] So they may, but this reduces them to the material of sociology. The methods of science can describe the *mores*, but this does not account for their hold over us, the moral imperative which we feel. Margaret Knight gives us a lot of detail about 'instinctual social responses' and the 'growing realisation of the extent to which gregarious animals exhibit co-operative, altruistic behaviour, not only towards sexual partners, and offspring, but towards other members of what can reasonably be called the community',[2] and she takes it for granted that animal behaviour provides the clue to human standards.

This is a popular theme among Humanist apologists. As man has developed bodily from the animals, so he has taken over animal instincts (social as well as anti-social, *pace* Morris and Co.) and then these social impulses have

[9] M. Ginsberg, 'On Justice in Society', quoted in review by I. C. Tipton in *Humanist*, December 1965. The review itself is a valuable insight into the Humanist view of morality.
[1] J. Huxley (ed.), *The Humanist Frame*, p. 37.
[2] Margaret Knight, 'Morality – Supernatural or Social?' in *The Humanist Outlook*, p. 47.

been refined by human social contact to the high level of awareness and responsibility we now enjoy. This theme comes up so frequently in their writing that it passes uncriticized as axiomatic. James Hemming talks of the 'new enlightenment, along with other advances in scientific understanding of the past two centuries, while undermining the absolutist foundations for moral values, has offered new foundations in their place – roots for human values in the creative process itself, and in the nature and needs of man'.[3] That 'creative' and 'nature of man' carry no Christian overtones is clear, as he goes straight on to give the evolutionary story: 'to develop the range of feeling in ourselves and encourage its development in others would seem, therefore, good by the evolutionary criterion . . . ' and later, ' . . . if we accept the evolutionary trend of greater individuation as a good thing . . . '. But what criteria of 'good' have we for this judgment? The confusion is endless. Whatever we are offered that is 'new' it is not 'new *foundations*'. It has been a commonplace among philosophers for centuries that 'ought' cannot be derived from 'is'. We may describe how things *are*; we may say what they *ought* to be; but these are two logically distinct areas of talk. 'Is' is molecule-talk and all ideas of blame or praise, good or bad, better or worse, are excluded. Yet Humanist writing, with its constant backlong glance at evolution, animal heritage and so on, crosses the boundary between 'ought' and 'is' over and over again without seeming to be conscious of doing so. Professor Anthony Flew devotes several lucid chapters of his monograph *Evolutionary Ethics*[4] to showing how 'is' and 'ought' are logically separate, and then appears to say that some sort of link must be supposed or else we can't get started morally. Pat Sloan, in *Humanist* for June 1968, writes of the efforts of Prince Peter Kropotkin to support 'Goodness without

[3] James Hemming, *Individual Morality*, pp. 24ff.
[4] A. Flew, *Evolutionary Ethics* (Macmillan, 1967).

God'. Kropotkin had ploughed much the same furrow as Mrs Knight: 'warfare in Nature is chiefly limited to struggle between different species, but within each species, and within the groups of different species which we find living together, the practice of mutual aid is the rule . . . '. Pat Sloan seems to think this will get morality clear of God-sanction, but wonders how it will work out in education. What should we say?

> 'Is it to tell a child that to be good is as natural as to be bad? . . . If the naturalness and satisfaction-giving quality of "good" behaviour can be established in early life as against the contemporary canonization through press and "entertainment" of thuggery, violence, crimes and sexual obsession, then surely a generation can grow up which sets a positive mean on social values and the present phase of agnostic nihilism may be overcome.'

But if the good behaviour is 'natural', rooted in instincts and animal ancestry, then, however convenient it may be, whatever survival-value it may have, it cannot be 'good'. We are simply back in molecule-talk again.

It must be said that Humanists have not really grasped this 'ought' nettle. One final example may be given. Dr Cyril Bibby in the opening essay of *Humanist Outlook*[5] raises the point as a 'common objection', but dismisses it in a line or two as resting upon 'linguistic ambiguity'. On the next page he gives examples of how rival 'private aims' might be dealt with and we read that 'another individual or society as a whole might reply with a contrary estimate of the consequences of such actions, and thereupon determine to use argument and/or social sanctions to discourage or present them'. What is the 'argument' to be based on? Do 'social sanctions' mean

[5] Cyril Bibby, 'Towards a Scientific Humanist Culture' in *The Humanist Outlook*, p. 13.

that the stronger group is going to win? We are soon left with references to 'happiness' and particularly the 'general happiness'. Bentham's 'greatest good of the greatest number' – and to Bentham 'good' meant 'happiness' – is always in the background. Arguments often end up in a Utilitarianism that argues that I ought to seek the common good because that is where my own good lies. This enlightened self-interest may be good practical politics, but it is certainly not the moral 'ought' since it makes my concern for others the expression of selfishness.

## Dangers of evolutionary ethics

### 1. Moral inversion

There is a danger in reducing morality to molecule-talk. The evolution-of-morals scheme has a backlash. Michael Polanyi writes of it in his criticism of Marxist theory. In Marxism, of course, morality is derived from economic and material forces. There is no separate, absolute 'ought'. Yet there is immense conviction. Polanyi describes this as 'moral inversion':

' . . . in such wise the traditional forms for holding moral ideas had been shattered and their moral passions diverted into the only channels which a strictly mechanistic conception of man and society left open to them. We may describe this as a process of *moral inversion*. The morally inverted person has not merely performed a philosophic substitution of moral aims by material purpose, but is acting with the whole force of his homeless moral passions within a purely materialistic framework of purpose.'[6]

Humanists would deplore this 'moral inversion' as much as anyone, but they have yet to produce a convincing apologetic which establishes man's fundamental

[6] M. Polanyi, *The Logic of Liberty* (Routledge, 1951).

moral convictions with a validity that is proof against Marxist reduction.

## 2. Who says what is 'good'?

Whatever difficulty Humanists may have in getting started, there is no doubt that they have plenty to offer in analysis and criticism of society. The criterion is 'what is good for man'. Baroness Wootton contrasts this with what she believes to be the Christian view: 'We no longer ask what is pleasing to God, but what is good for man.'[7] Christians believe that nothing pleases God more than what is good for man, but Humanists view the antithesis as a real one. So, while they find they can often work with Christians on social matters, they are afraid Christians may import some debilitating limitation from their faith at any moment.

The crucial areas raised by 'them' are the areas of individual freedom, and priorities in use of resources. If large numbers of people are to live together then severe limitations on individual choice are inevitable. If the maximum use is to be made of technical advance then large concentrations of people and capital are inevitable. The social machine both helps and hinders personal development. Living standards rise, in terms of spendable income, leisure, facilities, but this is at the expense of the lack of individuality and significance which has been referred to already. Who decides what liberties shall be allowed and what restricted? Consensus is the ideal, where people agree that certain things can be accepted and certain must be denied. Governments – and other agencies – attempt to create consensus and reduce conflict by explaining their intentions, the facts behind the decisions, allowing time for discussion and the forming of 'popular opinion'.

'Participation' is also an ideal, but has its limitations

[7] B. Wootton, 'Humanism and Social Pathology' in *The Humanist Frame*, p. 351.

as the problems get bigger and wider. At works level some progress may be made; at village pump level some things can be agreed upon, but a lot more are dictated by factors well beyond village control. At County Council level, participation is less still, and so on. Voting every five years or so, writing to MPs, joining pressure groups and lobbies seem small participations, but nevertheless represent unexpectedly powerful weapons against the bureaucratic mind. The organization of Western society is now exceedingly complex, an industry on its own. It is no place to rush in with slogans. Detailed and relevant knowledge is needed. Participation must be based on understanding, and freedom of speech is not the right to talk nonsense about things one knows nothing of. Yet to withdraw is to leave part of one's humanity. Humanists have often had cause to accuse Christians of doing just this, though there is now a welcome resurgence of Christian interest in social and administrative issues.

The results of the division of labour (see p. 37) need careful consideration. There is some evidence that the assembly-line technique is not best even judged on productive criteria. Some recent research suggests that pay and production bonuses are only one factor. 'Job enrichment' is the new phrase. Make the work more exciting, the work unit more matey, and production may actually *rise*. It is a pity that human values have to be sold under economic labels, but perhaps research here is pointing ways to more human working conditions. Another sphere is the relation between work and home – the area discussed by Symanowski in the comments referred to on p. 77. How can we avoid the situation where people live in different worlds at home and at work? What cross-links can be established in society? Maybe the mediaeval village community, centred on church and manor, was not as good as we think, and anyway cannot be brought back; but is there any new focus of integration? The TV gives us more news than was available in the market place, but not the same sense of belonging or mattering. I cannot do as much about Vietnam as I could do about people in need down the road.

Education is another field of wide concern. Humanists often see this as the key to the whole situation. Whatever hash may have happened in the past, at least a new generation can be reared by good education. This may sound horribly like conditioning and brain-washing. They would recoil at the thought. They only want the young taught to discriminate, to choose, to realize their freedom. There is a lively contemporary debate about education in which Christians are now taking a significant part.[8] They may be less sanguine than Humanists about the native goodness of children, but are certainly well aware of the implication for society of what goes on in schools.

All these raise problems of priority. Investment in industry, space research, war, education, housing, sociological research are competitors for the available resources. If man is viewed as producer-consumer then the priorities are weighted that way; research, education, even war will have to be justified as helping build up economic potential. In other times a high proportion of economic resources went into religious building, whether pyramids, Aztec temples or European cathedrals. This was an expression of priority, albeit often mixed with human pride and rivalry. What has taken over as chief spender? Motorways? Space vehicles? Universities? Perhaps there is no single new focus that might be the modern god, but a polytheistic collection of minor deities. Trailing along at the end come underdeveloped countries – lucky to get 1% of the Gross National Product of the wealthy West. Individuals and pressure groups composed of both Humanists and Christians batter

---

[8] See, *e.g.*, the educational journal *Spectrum* (obtainable from 47 Marylebone Lane, London W1) and *Learning for Living*, Journal of the Christian Education Movement.

away for more internationally just priorities; they deplore the concentration of economic power in the hands of a few international companies motivated mainly by profit and turnover; they deplore the nationalistic trends in some of the emerging countries themselves which make it hard to justify aid to them – garish public buildings and aircraft for new presidents at the expense of schools and transport. Perhaps they are making a small dent in the complacent, affluent, profit-worshipping West, and many individual projects have brought relief out of all proportion to the small amount wisely invested. Other projects have been a disastrous failure.[9]

Appeals to revise priorities again show a lot of enlightened self-interest. Underdeveloped countries are potential markets; if you don't help them they will soon multiply enough to rise against the West; they may (final threat) drift into the Communist camp. These are not the motives from which the Humanist or Christian sponsors really act. Why can they not sell their ideals of human dignity, equality of opportunity, right to share of world resources, straight? Christians may say human nature is basically biased to selfishness. Humanists have to do a tight-rope walk, blaming the past (colonial, Christian, or other) conditions for the present mess, but keeping faith in the basic decency and goodwill of human nature. Christians may have more to say, too, about the possibility of redemption and renewal, and also the idea that *God* is concerned in the matter. But that is for another chapter.

## Them–us–me–nature tension

The tensions outlined in the last two chapters can now be reviewed in the light of 'them'. Is it now a four-cornered fight? There are, as has been noted, very real

[9] See, *e.g.*, essays by Lord Ritchie Calder and Lord Boyd Orr in *The Humanist Outlook* for balanced statements by two distinguished Humanists closely connected with United Nations relief work.

tensions between 'us' and 'them'. 'Me-them' tensions are largely the same as these. The control of, and control by, nature affects 'us' and 'them' in different measure but in much the same ways. Perhaps the situation can be represented thus:

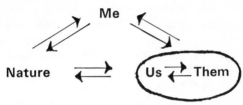

For the individual, the principal tensions are still the immediate limitations imposed by nature, and the social limitations imposed by us and them (in their different ways). The second of these makes for the most high feeling. As Rousseau said, '*things* do not rile us, only ill-will does'; I may accept my physical limitations, but economic disadvantage riles me because I feel 'they' could do something about it; my family are unreasonable and stop me doing what I want to. With my other hat on, when I am part of the 'us' or 'them' I may of course react much differently. X's objections are now selfish or unreasonable barriers to the common good. We and they may have our own disagreements about priorities but we are agreed that X's objections may be disregarded – or, on the other hand, we may take his part. Asylum is offered to a defecting Russian author or scientist, because the British 'them' thinks his individuality is being crushed by the Russian 'them'. (International consensus into a world-wide 'them' is exceedingly rare – help in earthquake or flood disasters are the nearest evidences.)

The great difficulty in this us and them versus me tension is knowing what standard to use. Who acts as umpire? There are always people whose only sanction is being 'found out'. Whatever they can get away with is right for them. The recent hippie commune is another attempt to break the tension – get away from it all and just be 'us'. Vastly developed technology has weighted the scales hopelessly against 'me'. Unless there is a powerful umpire, 'they' can do what they like. Here arises the whole question of the treatment of criminals. The very word 'treatment' begs the question. In times of the acceptance of absolute moral law, whether Christian, Roman or Greek, the question was one of punishment and justice, and often the punishment was more in evidence than the justice. Now the social sciences have shown us, quite properly, that many factors influence the evil-doer and mitigate his offence. But this approach runs riot so that 'evil-doers' no longer exist. In their place we have 'social deviants'. Humanism is particularly prone to this shift, since they are against 'absolutes' and their thinking drifts easily to scientific explanations. So Baroness Wootton writes of 'Humanism and social pathology', 'All societies have their misfits', and goes on to say how they should be dealt with:

' . . . the influence of Humanist attitudes upon every aspect of social pathology has indeed been remarkable. The norms of behaviour have been modified to suit Humanist conceptions of morality; toleration has been correspondingly extended; and – most striking of all – scientific method has invaded the field of penology, and perhaps even threatens to undermine traditional methods of dealing with malefactors.'[1]

So there has come the concept of 'treatment' rather than punishment. 'Retribution' is dismissed from penology as a crude survival of vengeance. The only factors are deterrence and reformation, and both these are up for scientific investigation of the most efficient ways. In all this, it is horribly possible that the humanity of the offender ('misfit') is squeezed out. He is a 'thing' that

[1] B. Wootton, in *The Humanist Frame*, pp. 347, 349.

'they' bring back into line, not a 'he' who has misused freedom of choice and suffers the 'just' penalty. There is no 'justice' in treatment, only efficiency. Christians believe that 'we' and 'they' stand under a higher court of judgment and can be called to account for the way individuals are dealt with, that there are fixed moral principles, and that 'just retribution' is not only a possibility but a duty. Humanists don't seem to want the depersonalization that 'treatment' suggests; much of their literature at least stands boldly for the individual. One is tempted to ask 'which individual?' The prisoner of conscience whom Amnesty helps gets their full support; so in principle does the Christian sent to a Russian prison for teaching his children (though he features less in their writings). They are genuinely against brainwashing and duress, but not clear how they avoid this excess and yet go in for 'social pathology'. As before, it is the getting started that bothers them. Once off the ground they have useful contributions to make. Christians could pay attention to these while still courteously pointing out the starting difficulty.

The other main tension is between them and nature. What control is possible or allowable? If the earth is the Lord's and the fullness thereof, then there is a landlord who might be expected to give advice on how to run the estate. But if man is on his own, is he limited only by his own ignorance? Reference has already been made to biological engineering – *Brave New World* gave an imaginary case-history – and there is more and more that can be done in agriculture, space exploration, transport, to 'set man's glory far'. Humanists applaud each advance, yet are also anxious to know who controls the new powers. They are well aware of the dangers of scientific power out of control, and see all too clearly the spectres of pollution and the rape of the earth.

If they have any fixed goal, it seems to be the survival of Man as a species, and this is certainly threatened by the present insensate consumption of the earth's resources. Pollution has taken over from the H-bomb as the Chief Enemy. Pesticides produce a new danger – cumulative poisoning as minute quantities of DDT or mercury build up to a lethal dose. Ecology is the 'in' science. Men are just beginning to realize the damage they are doing. Lake Erie supports no fish and it would take at least 100 years to put it right. British anglers fight a constant battle to keep a few miles of unpolluted stream. Even here the screams often come for economic reasons. The *Torrey Canyon* disaster shed tons of crude oil on British West Country beaches; the holiday trade was threatened, and protests mounted. The clearing operation involved thousands of tons of detergent, anything to break up the oil and clear the beaches. It also ruined the ecology of hundreds of miles of coastline, extinguishing species that will take decades for nature to replace. 'We are the masters now' is the proud boast of technological man. It may be a hollow boast; man may be digging his own grave.

But the more thoughtful writers show signs of deeper consideration, something akin to reverence. Is this the way men should treat their home? Are there no limits to avarice and pride? Our enormous know-how would have seemed to the Greeks rank *hubris*, the over-weening pride that must bring down the vengeance of the gods. James Hemming says that man is 'inescapably custodian of this planet' – but what can 'custodian' mean in the absence of someone who has entrusted us with the custody? The 'them-nature' tensions pose the same problems as 'me-nature' tensions, only writ larger. Survival seems a possible anchor, and features in much of the literature. But it will not stand analysis, and is hard to sell to the selfish. Why should they care about posterity? Why not a short life and a gay one?

## Another step to humanness

Does this wider society make for more or less humanity? 'Us' broadened humanity, developed powers of inter-relation, love, service and sympathy. Does 'them' do the same?

The question is focused in education – because here we are helping new human beings to develop. They are given factual information and some training in reason – an introduction to 'molecule-talk'. They are given opportunity to 'discover themselves', to experience choice, hope, joy, anxiety, and to express this in writing, art, drama. They are carefully helped in 'us' situations to develop co-operation, consideration, joy in company of others, sympathy and understanding. What about the wider field? They are being trained to take their place in the big wide world of 'them'. For this they are introduced to moral principles – the emphasis on sets of rules is less popular nowadays, and probably rightly so – moral principles to apply to the situations they will find themselves in. For most teachers, whether Humanist or Christian, these principles have some stability. However they are justified, they are presented as valid guides to conduct. Children are to be helped to a progressively coherent view of life, to act as a complete person, relating action rationally to a few high-level principles that are consistent among themselves. James Hemming gives these as reverence for the individual personality, respect for truth, honesty in dealings and relationships, responsibility for one's own actions, consideration of others, care and help for the weak and needy, open-mindedness to the ideas of others, responsible involvement in the long-term betterment of mankind. This is a list of values with which Christians could find themselves in hearty agreement. The extended list in *Individual Morality* (p. 59) is even fuller and reads like a commentary on the 'fruits' of the Spirit in Galatians 5.

H. J. Blackham says much the same thing:

'Morally[2] the fundamental thing is respect for human being in every person including oneself as autonomous and responsible. With this goes respect for rational standards in forming opinions and making decisions. With this self-dependence goes recognition of inter-dependence and acceptance of the conditions of coexistence and co-operation. Awareness of and response to the needs of others is as normal and approved as respect for their human dignity. Giving sense and value to all is the enjoyment of a personal life of one's own.'[3]

These are worthy ideals, a blueprint for humanity which is worth the struggle and tension. How will it be achieved? By explanation and example, by social reform, better living conditions, and so on. What barriers are there? That human beings seem to drag their selfish feet, that economic interests loom large, that advance brings new powers of exploitation. Christian and Humanist see this all too clearly. Blackham writes:

'Highly organized advanced industrial societies are likely to throw up a new type of gangster who may be the deadliest of all. Worse than the old theocracies may be the new technocracies. The technical expert and the efficient administrative official are first-class public servants, but as technocrats and bureaucrats who hog the decisions and manipulate men for the creation of some Brave New World, they would be the ultimate enemy. That particular essay in dehuman-ization for power is the last word in man's inhumanity to man. If these defaulters and gangsters are the real enemies of the humanists, their friends and allies are all those who rally against these enemies. If many of

[2] This cannot mean here 'according to the *mores*', but has the 'ought' sense.
[3] H. J. Blackham, *Humanism*, p. 208.

these happen to be Christian, who will be surprised? and who will mind?'[4]

C. S. Lewis devoted his essay *The Abolition of Man* to an analysis of 'man's control over nature' and shows how the power in the hands of the Conditioners leads eventually to the conquest of human nature:

'The ultimate springs of human action are no longer, for them, something given. They have surrendered – like electricity, it is the function of the Conditioners to control, not to obey them. They know how to *produce* conscience and decide what sort of conscience they will produce. . . .

For the wise men of old the cardinal problem had been how to conform the soul to reality, and the solution has been knowledge, self-discipline, and virtue. For magic and applied science alike the problem is how to subdue reality to the wishes of man: the solution is a technique.'[5]

Christians may suspect Humanists of having helped the new 'enemies' in: Humanists may suspect Christians of having league with similar enemies of magic and superstition. But in the educational aims mentioned above, they stand together against unreason and despair. They have this in common. They have their differences, of course, like how this will be achieved, and whether there is anyone to help. But that is for the next chapter.

[4] *Op. cit.*, p. 168.
[5] C. S. Lewis, *The Abolition of Man* (Bles, 1943), pp. 44, 52.

# 7 Anyone else?

## Is man on his own?

We have looked at increasing humanness. Man is more than molecules, naked ape, economic unit; more even than self-awareness. To be human is to live in groups and in society and to know the feelings, responsibilities and tensions this involves. Here we come to the end of the road as far as Humanists are concerned. 'Man is on his own', says their hand-out, 'and must solve his problems without the security or guidance of any absolute.' This, they plead, is as far as reason can take you. Beyond this you are in the realms of superstition, double-think and wish-fulfilments.

### *1. Is man reasonable?*

But 'reason' turns out to be an uncertain friend. It is notoriously difficult to define, and Humanists find themselves in a double difficulty. The first difficulty arises because of the evolutionary bias of their thinking. As C. S. Lewis pointed out in his essay 'Funeral of a Great Myth', it is only by reason that we understand the scientific world-view, formulate its laws, and infer what may have been before and what may come after. Reason is the keystone of the whole system, building upon deductions from scientific data to achieve what he calls the Great Myth, the whole sweep of evolutionary philosophy.

'But at the same time the Myth asks me to believe that

reason is simply the unforeseen and unintended by-product of a mindless process at one stage of the endless and aimless becoming. The content of the Myth thus knocks from under me the only ground on which I could possibly believe the Myth to be true. If my own mind is a product of the irrational – if what seem my clearest reasonings are only the way in which a creature conditioned as I am is bound to feel – how shall I trust my mind when it tells me about Evolution?"[1]

The evolution of wireless or the steam-engine has intelligence behind it. Some Christians would accept the evolution of man as the working out of God's intelligent purpose. Humanists cannot have this. How then can they authenticate reason? Must evolution get a capital 'E' and become a new god?

In the second place, wherever it arises, reason still poses a problem. Humanists often use it to mean 'relating to empirical evidence'. Conclusions are drawn from what is observed by the senses. Hence, they argue, disease and famine are to be attacked with the objective methods of science – inoculation, irrigation, *etc.* – and not with Canute-like declarations, or prayers. In this sense 'rational' is the way of the positivistic sciences – experiment, observation, deduction. On this understanding, religion is 'irrational'. You cannot perform an experiment to show that prayer is answered in the same way that you can show that cortisone disperses inflammation. Jesus himself was against such 'experiments' anyway.[2] But by the same axe, personal judgments, ethical judgments and aesthetic judgments are 'irrational'. You cannot perform an experiment to show that sunsets are beautiful or Wagner's music insolent.

In the heady days of Logical Positivism, A. J. Ayer (a

[1] C. S. Lewis in *Christian Reflections* (Bles, 1967), pp. 82ff.
[2] Mark 8: 11, 12.

recent president of the British Humanist Association) published his famous *Language, Truth and Logic*,[3] showing that religious language was (on his criteria) 'non-sense'. The sword was too sharp – it cut away everything except molecule-talk – and his second edition watered down the doctrine, and his more recent studies[4] expressly deny the sceptical conclusions that could be drawn from his earlier book. The sword is still too sharp. If 'reason' is restricted to this empirical approach, it leaves us only with impersonal molecules and forces.[5]

Humanists don't want it this way, and so they salvage the areas of personal, ethical and aesthetic discourse by defining 'reason' a little more widely. It is now used to mean 'relating to empirical evidence or consistent with the consensus of informed opinion'. There is no surrender to relativism. Everyone is not right. There are criteria in art and ethics as in science. It is 'unreasonable' to go against the generally accepted conclusions of those experienced in a given field. It therefore borders on 'common sense'. But the one 'sense' that has been 'common' – the one thing about which mankind has agreed for centuries – is that we are not alone. What the gods are like, what they demand, how they should be served or propitiated, have all been matters of dispute, but *that* they were a factor to be considered has been disputed only by small minorities. The man in the street may in fact join this 'common sense'. He persists in telling Gallup-pollsters that he believes in God, though he might not be regarded as 'informed' opinion. Yet, are

[3] A. J. Ayer, *Language, Truth and Logic* (Gollancz, 1936). The second edition (1946) contains a long preface replying to criticisms of the first edition.
[4] See, *e.g.*, A. J. Ayer, *The Problem of Knowledge* (Penguin, 1956), p. 68.
[5] For a detailed statement of this argument see, *e.g.*, John Macmurray, *The Self as Agent* (Faber, 1957) which sees Descartes' isolation of the thinking observer as the root of the trouble. Macmurray would substitute 'I *act* therefore I am', to preserve man in his wholeness. Macmurray's thesis is powerfully applied to modern theology in R. Blaikie, *'Secular Christianity' and God who Acts* (Hodder and Stoughton, 1970).

Humanists 'informed'? 'Evidence' depends upon the observer. If you want to be a scientist you must go and look, and expect to find causes and effects; if you want aesthetic experience, you must expose yourself to the art or music and expect communication, something beyond the paint or sound waves. And if you want religious experience you must be equally ready to listen sympathetically. The task of reason is to relate and codify the experience within each framework, to make it as coherent as possible, and to show what relation exists between the various ways of involvement in any given experience.

Christians may rejoice that Humanists are such apostles of reason. In a rootless, existential world, where many people are prepared to live by hunch or 'animal spirits', they should welcome people who say loudly and often that reason is man's strongest weapon, that argument is nearly always preferable to force, and the unexamined life is not worth living. Christians might even try to present their own world-view with a little more reason – as Peter exhorted his correspondents, 'be prepared to make a defence to any one who calls you to account . . . with gentleness and reverence'.[6]

## 2. Is Christianity reasonable?

Some Christians have tried this in a big way. There have been many who have echoed Isaiah's 'Unless you believe you will never understand', and have gone on from this truth to decry the use of reason. But there have also been many who have laboured to show the reasonableness of Christian belief. More than that, even, they have attempted to show by reason that God exists. The most famous attempt is Thomas Aquinas's 'Five Ways', and there have been many re-statements of the theistic arguments. Aquinas suggested that whenever you started looking at nature, you could be led logically to acknowledge that God is. The arguments seem very convincing

[6] 1 Peter 3: 15.

to believers – the argument from design, for example, as witnessed by the 'Fact and Faith' films, seems quite unanswerable, and believers are often a little downcast when it bounces off the reasonable unbeliever. It may be that such arguments have their place in confirming the faithful, and promoting points for discussion. They cannot produce logical certainty. For one thing, if they could, faith would vanish and the kingdom of heaven would be open to the clever folk who could follow the arguments most quickly.

The most that reason can do is to show that Christian belief is not inconsistent with other disciplines or knowledge, to show, in fact, that the Christian world-view is closely knit and need exclude no data. A most interesting feature of Christian intellectual experience is the excitement and solidity to which many have borne witness. Committing themselves to the God who is *there*, who reveals himself, they find their thinking, experience and interest broadened, and a new coherence and integration taking place in their view of the world.

### God-talk

*1. The integrating language*
This new experience and integration makes use of a different vocabulary. Just as 'me-talk' is different – perhaps you might say 'higher' – than 'molecule-talk', so 'God-talk' is higher than 'me-talk'. God is not a man who can be spoken of as one among many. Verbs of choosing, desiring, going, hearing and so on can be used only analogically of him. Thus we use terms like 'personal' and 'Father', but realize that our best human experiences are only shadows or hints of what is the character of God. So we may say of the most loving, caring, just father we have heard of, God is like that, only more so.

This difficulty of language dogs much discussion. Personal language may easily get devalued to molecule-talk. God-talk, much more easily, gets devalued to personal language. Some people have called God-talk myth – not meaning it is untrue, but that it is poetic, evocative language to carry abstract ideas in concrete form. Not just allegory, in which one 'thing' stands for another 'thing', but language that hints, suggests, puts you on the way to understanding what the reality must be like. So God 'dwells in unapproachable light', 'heard' the cry of this people in Egypt, 'sent' his Son to be the Saviour of the world. Some use myth in this sense, of the early parts of Genesis, seeing these records as telling us that the world is God's idea and that man has a worthy place in it, but has lost much of this privilege through his refusal to be bound by God's will. Others have resisted this strongly – as a sell-out to scepticism – and have tried to show that these records can be understood in a more concrete fashion. Art and music have been heavily drawn upon to communicate the mystery, grandeur and awe of God's character. The Byzantine icons and mosaics, for example, suggest something beyond ordinary experience, something larger than life, more demanding, more real. No wonder Humanists complain of the difficulty of God-talk, its lack of definition or openness to test.

Christians haven't always been at home with it, either interpreting it too literally or spiritualizing it all away. When Dr J. A. T. Robinson wrote his *Honest to God*, the *Observer* heralded it with an article headed, 'Our image of God must go'. He wrote of the difficulty of images of God 'up there' or 'out there', and the phenomenal sales showed that many of the bookish felt the same difficulties – though they may not have found the bishop's 'God in the depths of Being', 'the unconditioned in the conditioned', very much help to clearer understanding.

It may help to outline briefly here a possible way of looking at God-talk, by reference to our earlier 'three-cornered-contest' between nature-me-us-them. Each of these three areas has its own language, with its own presuppositions. Molecule-talk assumes a real world, cause and effect, and the significance of rational thought. Me-talk assumes personality, choice, emotion, freedom. Us/them-talk assumes some inter-personal 'ought', responsibility, duty. As we have seen, no one can be reduced to the others. Now 'God' cannot be fitted in among any of these. God is not subject to space and time limitations; he is not one person among many. Yet God-talk gives accounts of things that can be accounted for in the other fields. Thus Psalm 104 talks of God making the springs gush out in the valleys, though molecule-talk can give a perfectly adequate account in its own terms. In Psalm 51 David repents his sin against God, though us/them-talk would give an account in terms of wrong to Uriah and molecule-talk would give an account in terms of social deviance. Again, it is not surprising that the Humanist thinks Christians are inventing this God-talk when perfectly good explanations already exist. Certainly 'God' cannot be fitted into any of these three frameworks, nor can be go into a fourth area on the same level. It is possibly helpful to think of the three languages as sides of a solid, with God-talk across the top, like the top of a box:

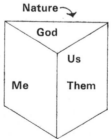

In this way, God-talk can have common lines of contact with each of the other three. Like the other languages, it has its own presuppositions – what philosophers call a self-revealing Absolute, or, as Hebrews has it, 'Whoever would draw near to God must believe that he exists and that he rewards those who seek him.'[7] His existence cannot be proved logically from other viewpoints, but Christians who have made the presuppositions and sought for God have found evidences of his activity, and have progressively found that God-talk makes sense. It also provides the support for all the other ways of looking at experience. The realm of nature, the molecule-talk area, is seen to depend upon God as creator in setting it going, and God as sustainer in keeping it going. It is regular and open to rational investigation because it is the work of a reliable, rational God. The personal area of 'me-talk' is another gift of God who has made man in his own image, able to choose and experience joy, sadness, hope and fear. The social area of us and them reflects God's providential care, setting people in society where personality may develop more fully and where collectively they can exercise dominion over the earth.

There have been many other attempts, especially recently, to show the nature of religious language. In various ways the writers have tried to show that God-talk is valuable, and introduces us to a fresh and fuller understanding of human possibility.

### 2. A problem for Humanists

Humanists remain unimpressed by all these attempts. To them the presupposition is a false one, a needless one, possibly even a ridiculous one. They cannot, of course, prove God does not exist, any more than Christians can give logical proof that he does. Their own presuppositions include the implied negative, and the one thing they seem to have in common across all their differences is agreement that man is on his own; there isn't anyone else. They argue among themselves whether they should be agnostic or atheist. The sterner spirits, such as the more militant minority who form the National Secular

[7] Hebrews 11: 6.

Society, want *Humanist* to be atheistic with no nonsense. The more moderate take various degrees of agnosticism, from the near atheistic, to the reluctant admission that 'you can't be sure'.

This lands them in the task of explaining why God-talk so permeates human language everywhere. This has to be done at two levels. First, why is mankind so incurably religious? Why does every language have so much God-talk in it? And second, how are we to account for the religious experiences of very many individual Christians and other religious people?

The Humanist reply in each case is, from the Christian point of view, another essay in nothing-buttery and reductionism. To the first question, they revert to their evolutionary motif. Religious interpretations of experience evolved along with aesthetic and ethical languages, as mankind confronted a big and wonderful world. In the last century, evolutionary progress was supposed from animistic beginning, through polydaemonism, polytheism, henotheism, to monotheism. Alternatively a start was found in magic, and Frazer's *Golden Bough* is still often reverently referred to as providing the secret of man's religious quest. The shift in philosophical emphasis over the last 100 years has made this less credible, but the major blow has come from anthropological evidence, such as Lang and Schmidt, which has shown that the steady upward pattern is most unlikely.[8] But the grand sweep of evolution, biological and now psycho-social, is axiomatic to Humanist thinking and so this type of 'explanation' comes out over and over again in their writings – usually as an aside (something everybody accepts), occasionally more explicitly:

'The earth was not created: it evolved. So did all the animals and plants that inhabit it, including our

[8] For a summary of this evidence see C. G. Martin, *Must Men Worship?* (Longman, 1969).

human selves, mind and soul as well as brain and body. So did religion. Religions are organs of psychosocial man concerned with human destiny and with experiences of sacredness and transcendence. In their evolution, some (but by no means all) have given birth to the concept of gods as supernatural beings endowed with mental and spiritual properties and capable of intervening in the affairs of nature, including man.'[9]

But such a sweeping, evolutionary explanation, as we have seen, explains everything *away*, reducing all, animal, man, society, religion, to molecule-talk.

Other reductions have been to personal terms, finding the origin of religion in fear. Man, lonely and afraid in his awesome world-home, invented spirits whom he could propitiate, or who might help him. These then developed into the clearer concepts of the great religions of the world. This derivation from fear is very old (it occurs in the writings of Polybius) but is full of difficulties. First it is hard to identify sheer funk, the fright that leads to flight, in human behaviour. The flight is always from what is seen as 'bad' to conserve what is 'good', so the knowledge of good/bad must be prior to the fear. Secondly, human fear often has a strain of fascination in it. This is the 'numinous' of Otto, the awesome interest in the unknown. Fear is too simple a term. Much has been made of Otto's 'numinous' and it certainly is an important factor in any religion. But Otto was investigating only the psychological basis of religion; he was not debating its truth. Is there a reality corresponding to the 'awe'? There is water to quench thirst, other people to meet our love of society. Is there anything to meet our numinous awareness? Do the heavens declare the glory of God, or are they just the occasion of a numinous experience? When Isaiah had his highly numinous

[9] J. Huxley in *The Humanist Frame*, p. 18.

experience in the temple, he felt he was confronted by an awesome Other – 'my eyes have seen the King, the Lord of hosts'.[1]

Where did the idea of God come from? Christians have the easy answer that it came from God, because he revealed himself to people, some of whom listened and found out. So they discovered the God who spoke to them. But Humanists cannot have this. For them, man must invent a God – either from fear, or from some other need.

The second hurdle is perhaps stiffer. What happened millennia ago, when mankind was young, is anyone's guess. But what happens now when some good friend of a Humanist – or even (as happens surprisingly often) some good Humanist himself – becomes a Christian? Professor H. A. Hodges tells us of an academic friend who, on hearing of the Professor's conversion, took a course of reading in Freud to find out what had happened. We have seen the open and sensitive reaction of some Humanists to this situation (p. 69). Others, perhaps less personally pressed, write more swingeing stuff. Christian conversion is an escape, a refusal to meet the awesome responsibilities of being alone. The mechanism by which it is produced is akin to psychological brain-washing. Billy Graham and his fellow-mass-evangelists are seen as expert mind-benders. Words like 'emotional', 'irrational', are thrown around. Occasionally there is the admission that the way of agnosticism is hard and that only the tougher minds can get along without some God-concept (this on different pages from those which say no-one believes in God nowadays) and so it is perhaps kindest, even necessary, to let religion survive for those who need it.

Very many Humanists have had (nominally) Christian pasts, and Christians would be better able to sympathize – and better able to avoid howlers – if they read of the relief Humanists have often found when they have renounced the 'outworn creed'. Bertrand Russell has

[1] Isaiah 6: 5.

written of this release, the new freedom he felt when he
finally renounced all supernatural aid (though he still
drew strength from the texts his grandmother had put in
the flyleaf of his Bible). David Tribe, swashbuckling
leader of the militant National Secular Society, has
spoken of the excitement of religious experience at sixteen and the disillusion when 'it goes cold on you' at
twenty, and of the relief at leaving it all. And many other
Humanists express their relief – sometimes at seeing
religion as a pleasant extension of the aesthetic (so that
they can enjoy Bach's music and religious art), sometimes
at being shot of the whole irrational business. 'Specifically religious emotions or experiences do not exist for us
to be excluded from. Religious emotions are simply
aesthetic ones which their owners have misinterpreted,'[2]
says Brigid Brophy.

Thus becoming a Christian can be reduced to molecule-talk (mass psychology) and being a Christian can be
reduced to personal me-talk (aesthetic experiences that
are 'misinterpreted').

Christian appeals to answered prayer, holy Scripture,
visions, charisma or whatever, are reduced to their appropriate category and God-talk again is shown to be
superfluous. The supreme communication from God to
men – the man Jesus Christ – occupies a lot of their
attention. Some dismiss him blandly as non-existent, and
asides such as 'if he ever existed' are stuck in to gall the
pious but not (I feel) to give serious information. Alle-
gro's mushroom myth was too wild for Humanist acceptance, but Professor Wells's more subtle 'enquiry' raises
the matter again – perhaps Jesus never existed.[3] But most
Humanists realize this is now a lost cause. Jesus, to them,
becomes a good, but misguided, man. Margaret Knight
doesn't even find him 'good', but a monomaniac shouting

[2] *The Humanist Outlook*, p. 195.
[3] G. A. Wells, *The Jesus of the Early Christians* (Pemberton, 1971). See
also Professor Wells's reply to various criticisms in *Humanist*, September 1971.

woes upon those who opposed him. Resurrection is staunchly refused. Such things just don't happen, and anyway plenty of *Who Moved the Stone?* – type of explanations abound.[4] Oddly enough, *Humanist* finds it hard to leave Jesus alone. One correspondent complained that 'this non-existent Jesus is the most talked-about person in your magazine'.

### 3. Some differences

'Argument weak: slang the plaintiff's attorney' – so runs an American legal proverb. It is perhaps unkind to apply it to Humanist apologetic (it could equally well apply to some Christian outpourings), but their writing on religious topics does give this appearance. Little attention is paid to difficulties of getting started, of justifying *their* belief in mind, reason, progress, responsibility; instead there is a great deal of party point-scoring, showing Christian faith and practice as either hypocritical, impossible, or ridiculous. It is these arguments that filter most easily to the less bookish, and they are met very much more widely in a rough, folk-lore form.

There is a steady polemic against miracle. This is partly a hangover from eighteenth- and nineteenth-century rationalism – the bland assurance, for example, of Renan that miracles just don't happen. Within Christendom, too, there has been a shift from mediaeval credulity, when any miracle was enthusiastically accepted, to a twentieth-century embarrassment when any miracle must be explained in psychological terms or demythologized. It is worth noting that Humanists are not impressed by the 'new' Christians who doubt or deny virgin birth, resurrection and the miraculous in general. 'It's rather like shadow boxing,' said Baroness Wootton, 'where one fights with people who will not stick to their

[4] F. Morison, *Who Moved the Stone?* (Faber, 1930), deals with various 'explanations' of the resurrection story. The book was originally conceived as a disproof of resurrection. The author ended by writing the exact opposite to what he originally intended.

own position. Probably what will happen is that if we sit back and let them get on with it the whole thing will die out in time.'[5]

If anyone starts with the axiom 'Miracles never happen' then, of course, every reported incident becomes the occasion of a search for what 'really' happened. No incident can be evidence for the miraculous since that is ruled out to begin with. But if you start with a more open mind, then each incident must be examined. For example, the question is not 'Can dead men live again?', but 'Did this dead man live again as recorded?' Then the records, the effect on witnesses, and so on must all be evaluated. You may not arrive at certainty but at least the question is not foreclosed from the start. If, in addition, the Christian presupposition of a God who reveals himself (a *positive* presupposition, note, not a negative fencing off of possible answers), then the investigation includes also 'what is being said by this event'. So Professor MacKay defines a miracle as 'an event in the natural world which comes to those present with the force of a revelation from God'. There is a considerable literature on the subject.[6] Christians could well do a bit of homework to enable them to 'give a reason' for this particular bit of their hope.

There is also a polemic – often a very angry one – against suffering. More specifically against a God who would allow it. Since Humanists accept no God, the polemic is, strictly, against Christians who are so depraved as to worship a God who (on their premises) must be responsible for suffering, It has been cogently put by writers throughout history. Voltaire's epitome, 'Either He is not good, or else He is not Almighty', sums up the indictment. The ancient world was a little more humble. Sophocles and others saw the tension but retained some

[5] From a speech at the Rationalist Press Association Dinner reported in *Humanist*, September 1968.
[6] *E.g.*, C. S. Lewis, *Miracles* (Bles, 1947; Fontana, 1960) and A. Richardson, *Christian Apologetics* (SCM, 1947), chapter 7.

awe, even a numinous reverence, in their response. There was anger and defiance, but there was greatness in it. The present Humanist apologetic has the greatness of man against insuperable (sorry, great) natural odds; but God is gone, so the highest tension and drama is missing. The mainspring of Greek drama has become merely a stick to beat Christians with. Christians, however, must brace themselves for the beating. They have no slick answer. Hinduism can slough off the problem of evil: good and evil are only appearances of the unchanging reality. The One is impersonal, inscrutable. But Christians are committed to a personal God who is the Father Almighty.

Again, a wide Christian literature shows that the problem is no easy one.[7] To summarize – and over-simplify – in a sentence: suffering caused by men is the price we pay for free will, and suffering caused by disaster is the price we pay for a fixed nature which we can understand and control. But the problem is deep and personal, often harder for those who try to help than for those who bear, yielding both triumphs of courage, devotion and patience, and horrors of despair, anger and blasphemy. Behind it lies the greater mystery, Whence evil? Is human freedom really worth the evil and suffering it has produced?

Humanists wrestle with no such mysteries. For them the whole subject is one more nail in the 'God' coffin. Yet they are left with the opposite problem, Whence good? and their evolutionary answers are not particularly convincing. Their stick may break at the end since they cannot establish standards of 'good' by which to declare suffering 'evil'. Without God, they are in danger of being without mystery. Being in charge of the world, they must rush on as best they know how. If 'happiness' is the goal (though not all Humanists are pleased with the 'happy man' symbol), then abortion, euthanasia and drugs can

[7] E.g., J. Hick, *Evil and the God of Love* (Fontana, 1968); H. E. Hopkins, *The Mystery of Suffering* (IVP, 1959).

eliminate or mask many occasions of suffering. But shall we lose with them as many occasions for courage, research and battle against disease, as many opportunities for care and devotion which Humanists also rate highly? *Brave New World* gave a moving picture of the 'misfit' in such a suffering-free society. But the pain and tension of this attack is real. It is a pity that Humanists rush to brandish it as a weapon, venting on their fellow-humans the pent-up anger they cannot lay before God. As Alan Willingale wrote in his review of *The Humanist Frame*, 'The doctor fails to raise this Job-like statement to a religious utterance because, although he asks the right questions, he puts them to the wrong person. If he humbly put these questions to God, not himself, he would be in the way of getting a true answer.'[8]

Christians may polish their weapons on the miracle front; they may bow humbly, hopefully and worshipfully before the mystery of suffering; but in their third stick, the Humanists have a much surer weapon. Before the charge that Christians have a lot of suffering and hypocrisy to answer for, they can do little but say 'sorry'. A belated 'sorry' to those they have cruelly wronged;[9] 'sorry' to those who, by reason of this dark record, find the way to faith more difficult; and 'sorry' to God, whose name has been blasphemed among the nations because those who named his name with their lips denied it by their lives. Humanists are often very decent about all this and produce it only when Christians drive them to it by keeping on about the good Christianity has done. The more militant (especially the National Secular Society) go in for bishop-bashing and are not short of material. Margaret Knight's pamphlet 'Christianity, the Debit Account' is a typical handout, and more lengthy works have no difficulty in dredging up every kind of excess –

---

[8] Sir R. Platt in *The Humanist Frame*, pp. 369, 370, reviewed by Alan Willingale in *Inter-Varsity*, Autumn 1963.
[9] As, *e.g.*, in the decree of Vatican II concerning persecution of the Jews, and the prayer of Pope John in this connection.

the bad popes, religious wars, the Inquisition, witch-hunts. Fruity titles such as 'The day a nun saw red' give testimonies against the church as potent as anything that appears on the other side in the evangelical press. Persecution is not so rife now, but current events give plenty of fuel. In some cases there is of course exaggeration, but not enough to make the stick much less weighty. There is no defence. The only honest thing for Christians to do is to submit to the belabouring – with the additional pang that God has been misrepresented; we have sinned, we and our fathers.

But sticks only break bones, not arguments; they may dent skulls, but not the truth. Even as they endure, Christians may reflect that this assault is doomed to failure. It is not difficult to show that many Christians have acted selfishly, wickedly, foolishly. But this proves little. If God does not exist, then he does not exist for anybody, and Humanists have taken on the Herculean task of showing that every single man or woman who ever claimed to live by the grace of God was mistaken. They cannot admit any single devoted Christian life to be evidence of 'Anyone else' able to guide, help or strengthen. Christians may also wish to make a distinction between those who profess and those who are truly committed to Christ. Many Christians would argue that the partnership between church and state under Constantine, and its subsequent development in the Middle Ages, was the biggest disaster ever. The true faith was lost in a mass of socially acceptable compromise. 'Their fruits' was one criterion that Christ himself proposed. This won't get them off the hook entirely, but does remind the stick-wielders that human greed and insincerity operates under many labels. Karl Popper sees this clearly:

'It was Robespierre's rule of terror that taught Kant, who had welcomed the French Revolution, that the most heinous crimes can be committed in the name of liberty, equality and fraternity: crimes just as heinous as those committed in the name of Christianity during the Crusades, the various eras of witchhunting and the Thirty Years' War.'[1]

Nor need Christians forget entirely the good that has been done. The world is strewn with hospitals, schools, universities, which were started by Christian initiative. In many cases these are now run by secular states, many of whose leading figures were trained in Christian schools. There is, of course, an Agnostics Adoption Society and a few homes for delinquents and the elderly are run by Humanists. It is also true they see their role more as stimulating governments than providing fire-brigading, stop-gap services. Yet the point was powerfully made by Trevor Huddleston in his TV interview with Lord Ritchie Calder. All this social betterment – which Lord Calder gratefully acknowledged – was, said the Bishop, the *incidental* effect of the gospel. The nineteenth-century missionaries did not go to Africa to set up hospitals, schools, *etc.*, but to tell men of the love of God. It surely carries rationalization too far to say they were mistaken in their mainspring; to ascribe the fruit to some other root. The more the argument is pressed, the more the rejection seems *a priori*. It cannot be that they were motivated by the love of God, *because* we cannot admit the serious possibility that God exists.

## Positive or negative?

Up to this chapter, Christians and Humanists have found much to agree about. True, Christians keep wanting to import 'foundations' to ideas of responsibility which Humanists take as axiomatic; Christians may also want to import revelation – that the Bible is not just 'good advice' but authoritative as a manufacturer's hand-

[1] K. Popper in *The Humanist Outlook*, p. 291.

book. But they want to say the same things about humanity including appreciation and control of nature, freedom, choice, care for others, mutual enjoyment in society. In this chapter however, there is a parting of the ways. Is there anyone else? Christians respond positively: Yes, the God and Father of our Lord Jesus Christ, who can be known, trusted, served in perfect freedom. The Humanists, perhaps characteristically, find themselves with a negative: No, it is useless for man to look for supernatural aid. Hence all Christian evidence must be reduced to some other category. They must guard the gates against the Hound of Heaven. But if they are wrong, then surely they are truncating man, robbing him of his highest possibility.

As a *Humanist* editorial put it, the exploration of common aims must not blind us to the fact that we eventually face each other across a great divide. Arguments and other missiles fly – fast and furiously in the polemical environment of university and college; occasional sniping in more task-centred groups of later life. This is not the ideal setting for better understanding. Professor MacKay wisely comments,

'What the Christian and the non-believing humanist need to do, then, is not to compete in terms of slogans, but to get together to hammer at the question of *evidence*, so that it becomes clear in what ways the Christian gospel claims to be *testable* in the sense of having consequences in daily life for the individual.'[2]

If argument *that* God exists is inconclusive, further progress may still be made by Christians trying to explain their understanding of *what* God is like. In Micah's words, 'What does the Lord require of you?'

[2] D. M. MacKay, *Humanism Positive and Negative* (IVP, 1966), p. 12.

# 8 What does God require?

**Has the church issued a fraudulent prospectus?**
If Humanists have got the wrong idea about what God is like and what his service means, they have considerable excuse. The less bookish have still more excuse. The 'church' has spoken with so many different voices, adopted so many different poses and laid such different emphases that the man in the street may well think it is irrelevant to him, and the bookish find all in confusion.

From some hand-outs one would judge that God's essential demand is for correct cultic behaviour; church attendance, particularly at Easter and Christmas, is the absolute minimum. At the other extreme, social involvement is the key; church-going or doctrine is an optional extra. Others again fight over doctrinal formulations – the vital thing is to say the right form of words. Since all this often goes along with normal human fallibility and selfishness in ordinary behaviour, the man in the street has some cause to think it doesn't matter, and the Humanist, already heavily involved socially, may well think he already has whatever is useful in Christianity.

It is, of course, easy and unhelpful to parody the muddle of communication – and the worse muddle of convictions and traditions – that have characterized most groups of Christians. But it must be frankly admitted that many grossly fraudulent prospectuses have been offered to the public. Two major faults may be noted. At one end, God is shown as demanding that men and women win or earn his favour by their good deeds (often narrowed to ceremonial correctness and decent living). Salvation is definitely by works. The stakes used to be high – a very real heaven and an equally real hell; but both these (especially the latter) have been devalued of late. At the opposite end there has been such an emphasis on justification by faith that an easy 'believism' has flourished in which acceptance of statements of faith is enough, with frequent neglect of any emphasis on the way of life the 'converted' should lead. In between there has grown up a muddled middle, suggesting that decency is enough, and everything will be all right in the end. The stern either/or of the gospel becomes a beneficent universalism. The Lion of the tribe of Judah becomes a household pet.

### An old problem
This is not a new situation. It was in full spate in 700 BC when Micah found wealthy landowners oppressing the poor farmer yet happy in their ritual 'worship'; priests avaricious; prophets prepared to say anything as long as their bellies were full; all kinds of religious practices being followed, even to the excesses of infant-sacrifice. Micah's outburst is the classic summary of the Hebrew prophets:

> 'He has showed you, O man, what is good;
>> and what does the Lord require of you
> but to do justice, and to love kindness,
>> and to walk humbly with your God?'[1]

There is nothing negative about this. Three strong, positive, demands. Humanists could welcome the first two – the justice and loyalty that are the key to a free and open society – but though they might be in favour of humility, they cannot walk humbly with God.

Micah's message did not stop the rot. The ritual ob-

[1] Micah 6: 8.

session and legalism remained a characteristic of Judaism, though justice, mercy and humility were not unknown. Jesus emphasized the prophetic message: 'Go and learn what this means, "I desire mercy, and not sacrifice".'[2] He also emphasized the inward disposition rather than outward action, and spoke afresh of the possibility of walking humbly with God, a God who could be known as Father, and whose forgiveness and fellowship he had come to reveal.

## Christian belief: giving in or coming home?

Humanists do not see it this way, however. Many have had a mild inoculation in institutional Christianity and see only the ceremonial and the rules. Whether these are relevant or not, they are seen as curbs on human freedom. The image of God they see is not of Father, but of boss – the Victorian paterfamilias made seven times hotter. Reconciliation with such a God is no boon to them. First, they sense no breach, and secondly they see 'repentance' as submission. Here, at the threshold, they find insuperable barriers.

H. J. Blackham expresses their objection clearly – and incidentally shows that he understands the Christian demand more clearly than some of its salesmen:

'Now Christ as a human personality is an enigma, but as a standard and pattern there is no doubt or obscurity about him: he is the archetype of unqualified submission and obedience to the will of God, the God of Abraham and of Isaac and of Jacob. It is impossible to follow Christ on any other terms, and the humanist finds acceptance of these terms a violation of himself and his whole experience. His rejection of Christ is therefore categorical: he can do no other.'[3]

[2] Matthew 9: 13.
[3] H. J. Blackham (ed.), *Objections to Humanism*, pp. 17, 18.

Here is the crunch. 'Lord, I'm coming home', sang Beverly Shea. 'A violation of himself', says Blackham. There is no baulking the issue that God's claims are real. Jesus and his apostles spoke of repentance just as surely as the Hebrew prophets. At root, repentance is a change of outlook, the taking of a new mental stance, the change from a self-centred outlook to a God-centred outlook. It may be a sudden realization, or a slow crumbling of self-trust and self-concern, but the springs and directions of life are changed. Jesus is *Lord*. Humanists are right to brush aside any watered-down version which suggests that repentance is an outmoded word, and that most people are all right really. Mr Blackham, at least, sees that obedience and reverence are central. Following Christ is not a euphemism for doing what I think best.

But – and this is the crucial question – is this man's highest possibility, or his lowest sell-out? In the parable, the prodigal son 'came to himself' when he decided to go home and say 'I have sinned'. He was truer to himself, more of a man, than when he lived as though his father did not exist.[4] This is not a grovelling attempt to buy off an angry God, but the only possible way of re-establishing relation with a God ready to pardon, full of mercy and truth. If we are wrong, then the truthful thing is to say so. And pardon is a two-way process. Forgiveness must be received, and this involves admitting it is needed.

## Sin: neurosis or realism?

Humanists are perplexed, not to say irritated or even amused, by the Christian's confession of sin. James Hemming, for example, is not impressed with Isaiah's confession 'Woe is me, for I am a sinful man' – 'it sounds like an excuse, to which the answer is, "You're not *only* a sinful man: why not get up and get going?" '[5] Why not, indeed! Isaiah did, in fact, do just that, *after* he had the

[4] Luke 15: 11–24.
[5] J. Hemming, *Individual Morality*, p. 85.

conviction of forgiveness and the divine commission. A very real part of the Christian's 'sense of sin' is precisely that he wants to get up and get going but finds he cannot. There is the additional pressure that 'sin' is not just wrongdoing against some other human being; it is the refusal of God's will. And though this may only slowly become part of the mental furniture of the believer, it must make him see things much more seriously. This *can* become neurotic; people can indulge in orgies of self-condemnation. And pastors and counsellors of all descriptions often have to try to help people distinguish false from true guilt. But not all guilt can be dissipated, and the reverse error of not worrying enough is far more common. At least, the Christian message is primarily *good* news. Those who are sick find there is a physician; sinners are told repentance is possible; and healing and forgiveness are a major theme of Christian praise. It is the confidence of acceptance that is the spring of the new life.

How do Humanists cope with their sense of failure (not, of course, in the absence of God, their sense of 'sin')? H. J. Blackham again is frank:

'What are the resources against this deterioration of attitude, which will help fortify and maintain humanist responsibility? If one is realistic and active from the start, if one comes early to terms with one's own guilt and failure, if one is content to think in terms of better and worse possibilities and not in black and white, if one strives for improvement and learns from results, good and bad, to do better, and if one thinks that a lot of effort for a little improvement is worth while, then one is insured against despair, then one has done the best one can to keep one's grip and to keep sane and to achieve the serenity of enjoyed experience. Otherwise, one condemns oneself to a more or less sick and sorry life, tolerable only in so far as one is able successfully to hide from oneself and others and to make do with make-believe.'[6]

This is honest stuff, facing feelings frankly. Better, no doubt, than Aldous Huxley's suggestion in *The Humanist Frame* that we should try to eliminate the 'deeply-rooted conviction of sin [*sic*]' by the use of drugs. Christians may still wonder if 'letting bygones be bygones and learning from mistakes' is really enough for the crises of life, or even its average experience. And they would have to say, too, that Mr Blackham has not yet reached the real depths of Isaiah's experience, the piercing realization that it is *God* we confront, not our neighbour or our ideal selves.

## Self-denial

### *1. Is self-denial human?*
It is not only at the threshold that there is trouble. Humanists are concerned to count the cost, too. The going on in Christian practice does not appeal to them either. It is not, they feel, just an initial grovel to get into God's good books. It is the start of a *life* of submission. This is often crudely traced; there is a strong strain of asceticism in Christian history (and most other religions) and Margaret Knight, for instance, has no difficulty in quoting from Thomas à Becket, Suso, St John of the Cross, Pusey and others to show the rigours people have undergone to 'save their souls'.[7] Many well-meaning people needed the words of Luther's friend: 'Brother Martin, you can't help your soul by hurting your body.' Again it may be said that ascetic excess is not the failing of our own age. Also we are not bound to approve all that has been done by great believers of the past. We may even point out that Jesus was condemned as frivol-

[6] H. J. Blackham, *The Humanist Himself* (Ethical Union, 1961), p. 8.
[7] *The Humanist Frame*, p. 429.

ous by those who liked the asceticism of John. Some modern (not to say 'mod') churchmen are bending over backwards to say the world is for enjoyment, and Christians need not go in for all this ascetic stuff.

Humanists are not impressed with this re-furbishing of Christianity. They suspect a faith that makes no demands, has no bite, and sells itself, like breakfast cereals, on big smiles and the good life.

They are familiar at least with enough of the New Testament to know that Jesus spoke of a man 'denying himself, taking up his cross and following me',[8] and they have been bashing away at the first few Beatitudes ever since Charles Bradlaugh wrote his diatribe *Are the poor blessed?* 'Is poverty of spirit even a virtue at all? Surely not. Manliness of spirit, honesty of spirit, fulness of rightful purpose, these are virtues; but poverty of spirit is a crime.'[9]

It is all very well for Christians to say people don't like this teaching because the shoe pinches. Self-denial may clip selfish wings or cut the bank balance. Many of the Humanist objectors are *not* particularly selfish – unless self-sufficiency be selfishness – nor gross materialists. Christians must take the objection on its own grounds. Does self-denial reduce humanity? What does it mean anyway? H. J. Blackham poses the question sharply:

'If one denies oneself, not symbolically as in Lent nor marginally by pushing half-a-crown into the tin of a Salvation Army Lassie on the appropriate day, but radically and in earnest, the well is poisoned: it is an ultimate wrong. To treat oneself as a means only to the ends of others, as to treat others as only means to one's own ends, is to destroy the source of value. There

[8] See Mark 8: 34.
[9] Quoted in *What they've said about the 19th Century Reformers* (OUP, 1971), p. 121.

has been a Universal Declaration of Human Rights. They are not strictly "rights" and may not even be "claims", but they are indefeasible dues if all human beings are to be recognized and accepted as human beings.'[1]

Without pressing again the question as to the 'source' of values or the nature of 'indefeasible dues', we must take seriously this demand to clarify the Christian claim. 'An ultimate wrong' says Blackham; 'essential' said Jesus. Are they talking about the same thing? If so, there is indeed a 'great divide'.

## 2. *The New Testament account*

Humanists suspect sudden conversions – they are written off as being the result of psychological pressure – and, to be just, many Christians suspect them too. They do happen, though, and persist much more often and much more successfully than the objectors or suspicious might allow. The slower, more thoughtful turning to Christ is less dramatic, and perhaps therefore less noticed. Among the bookish there is a tradition of decent moderation and 'Hallelujah' is an unusual word, so perhaps the drastic nature of conversion is less obvious. But just as feeding the 5,000 altered the time-scale and pressed the wonder of growth and harvest upon people's attention, so the occasional dramatic conversion may make the point that the most steady, decent, cultured turning to Christ imaginable is in fact an upheaval in the personality. Which is just as well, since nothing less is going to bridge the gap between the 'ultimate wrong' and the 'essential'.

Paul writes at length about this in 2 Corinthians 5 where he speaks of ontological change (that is, a change in 'how things basically are') and of two ways in which this works out. If anyone is in Christ, he says, there is a new creation. The powers, standards and possibilities of

[1] H. J. Blackham, *Humanism*, pp. 77f.

the new age have secured another bridge-head. A new power point has been connected to the mains. This is God-talk with a vengeance. The New Testament rings with it: he saved us; he has given us his Spirit; Christ has 'laid hold' of us; we are delivered from the dominion of darkness and transferred into the kingdom of his dear Son; we are born again and have eternal life. Hence Christian praise resounds with what God has done for us – an odd contrast to the Humanist preoccupation with the limiting demands God seems to make upon Christians. Of course this God-talk sounds artificial and nonsensical to the Humanist. Even while he listens to it (which he does rarely) he is automatically translating it furiously into personal or molecule-talk, thinking of psychology, indoctrination, environmental pressures that might account for this strange language. Jesus and Paul were blunter. 'Why do you not understand what I say? It is because you cannot bear to hear my word.'[2] 'The unspiritual man does not receive the gifts of the Spirit of God, for they are folly to him, and he is not able to understand them because they are spiritually discerned.'[3]

Humanists object, quite understandably, that this is high-handed, arrogant stuff. We may quibble about the adjectives – Christians do not 'arrogate' to themselves what is not theirs – but must say that if this is how things are, it must be stated. The nearest analogy is the statement that blind people cannot join discussions about colour. 'Are we blind also?' asked the Pharisees, and their pride hindered them from the admission that would have brought revelation. However nonsensical, or even irritating, it sounds to our non-Christian friends, we have to maintain that this is the true 'divide'. We must continue with all charity, and with all care to communicate as best we may, but to withdraw this basic division is to add confusion to confusion.

[2] John 8: 43.
[3] I Corinthians 2: 14.

### 3. New drive, new outlook

But, they may object, what's all this got to do with self-denial? It's the old red herring, dragging in God-talk when the question is a very earthy one of living in a very earthy world. Paul is not as unearthly as his critics suggest. Having stated the basic foundation – a new creature, the bridge-head established – he gives two ways in which this works out. Both these are extremely relevant to the self-denial question. He mentions 'the love of Christ controlling us' and a new viewpoint. A fresh emotional drive and a fresh intellectual approach.

Blackham sees self-denial as the 'ultimate wrong' because he sees it as making oneself 'the means only to the ends of others'. But love transforms the 'only'. Love desires the good of the other. The desired 'end' is not grudgingly accepted but freely followed and, paradoxically, this yields in practice the *growth* of personality of the servant, not its diminishment. This is the common experience in friendship and marriage – though cynics debunk, and failures disappoint – where service is freedom and delight. The love of Christ extends this to a wider circle, different in scope but not in kind, and not bare talk, but demonstrated in an example of concern, truth and devotion. 'Love' no longer stands without content. 'As I have loved you' gives the pattern. It is more demanding, often more perplexing, than any comparable personal relationship, but glimpsed by saints, apostles, prophets, martyrs, and many others. The Exley Report[4] – by two agnostics – frankly gives evidence of much nonsense, but also much of this truly loving service in CMS missions in Africa. Sister Theresa serves the poor of Calcutta, and George Burton served Canning Town. All would claim that 'the love of Christ controls', would refuse to credit it to their own temperament or dedication, but would rejoice that 'God's love is poured into our hearts by his Spirit which he has given us'.

[4] H. and R. Exley, *In Search of the Missionary* (CMS, 1970).

The other outworking of this 'new creation' is the change in mental stance. 'From now on, therefore, we regard no one from a human point of view; even though we once regarded Christ from a human point of view, we regard him thus no longer.'[5] The Authorized Version translation has given rise to the idea that Paul didn't want to know about the human Jesus, and this gets quoted from book to book, especially to show that Christianity is really a 'spiritualized' extract which rests on doubtful historical foundations. Paul is, in fact, as the Revised Standard Version (quoted here) makes clear, basing things firmly upon facts, but facts viewed from a different viewpoint. Before his dramatic encounter with the love of Christ he had the standards of judgment of the ordinary educated man of his day. Jesus was a potential leader to be feared and, as a Pharisee, Paul saw the threat to the established system. It seemed sensible, therefore, to join in the effort to eradicate the new, misguided sects. But now, a change of view! The 'new' had come, and the pieces of the jig-saw needed drastic rearrangement, so drastic that it took a year or two in Arabia re-thinking the whole business. But the new picture possessed a cohesion, a beauty and a power that his previous training had never provided. In this picture, not only Christ, but everyone found a fresh place. The barriers of class, race, sex and culture disappeared. People were no longer viewed 'from a human standpoint' of wealth or status, but as brothers for whom Christ died.

This is the key to 'self-denial'. It is implicit in the invitation of Jesus, where it is the start of 'following'. Following him means having a new focus, to see things in a new light. It is not being driven or towed. 'Following' is a voluntary activity. Undoubtedly this is a complex business. The disciples were not philosophers – though some of them were men of the world – and they submitted Jesus to no subtle cross-examination. But his

[5] 2 Corinthians 5: 16.

teaching and his life and his person wove together a self-authenticating claim. They lived with him and the memory of that living stayed with them. 'We were eye-witnesses,' says Peter. 'We behold his glory,' says John, a comment which he expands in his first Epistle, 'we have heard . . . we have looked upon and touched with our hands, concerning the word of life – the life was made manifest, and we saw it'.[6]

Humanists may find this incomprehensible, frustrating, time-wasting. Perhaps this is the core of Isaiah's and Augustine's paradox 'Believe and know'. From the outside, such an attitude must seem 'poisoning the well'. Phrases like 'intellectual suicide' are thrown around. But at least there is evidence that many people have found it the true development of their humanity. In their own experience they have found how right Paul's priorities are. For, as Humanists find with exasperation, his new awareness of human equality, the desire to serve, and all the social implications, are secondary to his main purpose: Be reconciled to God. So we are back again to the Huddleston-Ritchie Calder discussion. The new viewpoint puts relation to God right at the top of the charts, and from this deduces relationship to others and to the earth.

### 4. The willing response
The change of viewpoint has far-reaching effects, but few greater than this transformation of 'ultimate wrong' to 'glad service'. The New Testament rings with thanksgiving and praise to God who has granted us this privilege, adopting us into his family, empowering and commissioning us for his service. The bookish struggle with it at the articulate, intellectual level. Their reductionist techniques are always at hand to explain things away in terms of self-interest, Freudian complexes, social syndromes, and much else. They may well welcome a shift

[6] 1 John 1: 1, 2.

of goal from materialism and ostentatious wealth to social concern and cultured self-development – to this extent they are the Christian's allies; but the shift to Paul's goal 'that I may know him and the power of his resurrection' they deny categorically.

The non-bookish have a fairly small repertoire of arguments, sometimes superficial, sometimes the clearest distillation of human experience. But at the level of everyday life, they are very judges. Cynicism and debunking abound, but behind the banter, sincere Christian love carries its message. They are not insulated by status or education from the realities of living. They have no studies to retreat to. The Christian message of service, joy and hope lived among them is the sermon to which they will listen. Here it is 'open to test' before judges who know success from failure in the test. Most of them don't want to 'be done good to'. Materially they are affluent by comparison with their parents. It is difficult to see what the Humanist message, with its largely verbal form, can be for them. The Christian message, too, often seems irrelevant and wordy. But it need not be, and often isn't. Far more frequently than its friends or enemies realize, hope, joy and power for living are radiated and men and women are reconciled to God and to each other. Especially abroad in such awakenings as those in Africa, Indonesia and South America this pattern persists – not demand, but glad discovery and acceptance of God's offer in Jesus mediated through his people.

Throughout this there runs the golden thread of hope. We have not looked very closely at the Christian's hope, object of the Humanist's highest scorn, caricatured as 'pie in the sky when you die'. To this we must turn.

# 9 For better or worse?

## Man at the end of his tether?

If all we knew about man was the work of the mid-century playwrights of Europe, we should think him a very doubtful risk – treacherous, lecherous, selfish, arrogant, a mass of inhibitions and frustrations; above all, tired, very tired, playing out tired answers to eternal questions, unable to break through. Seeing the folly and evil of war, he still wars; knowing the desert of isolation in the city, he still cannot communicate; needing above all things love and acceptance, he makes it impossible by his antagonism and inability to accept himself. Humanists gloat over the emptying churches. They don't really like the playwrights' preaching the church's message of original sin very much, either. When, at the end of his life, their own prophet, H. G. Wells, wrote the despairing *Mind at the End of its Tether*, they detected that the great mind was cracking under the strain of a long life, not that the great mind had finally seen the truth, and come to a true, though pessimistic, conclusion. Humanism must be a philosophy of optimism; a success story with a happy ending. Evolution with a capital E has smuggled in, not only quasi-personal ideas, but hopeful ones too. We are on the up-and-up. True, there is every now and then a look over the shoulder to warn that progress is not automatic. Man is in charge. He has the tools at his disposal to push forward the great march to the Golden Age of human brotherhood. Do not falter now.

What if he does? What if he uses the tools to wreck his planet home? Oh, shut up! He mustn't! He won't!

Humanism is certainly optimistic, not just in bald, materialistic terms, but in terms of quality of life and relationship. Progress in this direction is not as small as the Jeremiahs believe. In Britain the Welfare State has done a lot. In some countries abroad the standard of living is low, but more people know it is low, and some are doing something about it. Anyway, they may argue, isn't this really what the church was talking about fifty years ago? The 'social gospel' reacted against 'pie in the sky' as sharply as did Marx. As heaven became less credible or desirable so the church's message became more earthly. No longer preparing people for judgment and the world to come, it set about the world we live in. Humanism has made a takeover bid for this enterprise, and the process of secularization is now well advanced in Western Europe and America. The welfare services and many agencies are no longer nominally Christian. Governments undertake the improvement of social conditions for Christian and new pagan alike. Christians cannot corner the social betterment market.

And yet we may wonder whether secularism has in fact taken over only a bankrupt firm. Are dividends being paid out of diminishing Christian capital? Some Christians think so, and say so perhaps a bit too confidently. Some even regard the secular social betterment industry as a rival concern and regret its success – a pity, since, whatever may be missing from the secular programme, it includes a great deal that provides people with valuable equipment for the human enterprise. Christians might more profitably see themselves complementing it, either from within the service or outside, with the specifically Christian ingredients of judgment and love.

Still the problem of optimism or pessimism remains. What of the future? How do the non-Christians see it?

Most of the non-bookish are prepared to live a day at a time, insure for some things, risk the rest. As to the distant future, they are occasionally alerted by a TV programme on pollution or war, but react with the hedges that either it'll be a long time yet, or there's nothing we can do about it. They may be concerned about the world their children will live in, but again this is less closely-knit than formerly. Children are more independent nowadays, and must look after themselves. Some of the older folk in this group do express concern and bemoan the passing of days when, they feel, standards of honesty were higher and the sense of belonging in the work group was more real than it is now.

The bookish take a longer view. They are the folk who get worked up about pollution and war. Humanists in particular, since the survival of the race features high on their list, must be concerned about developments that will use up all resources too quickly or make the place too dangerous or dirty to live in. The population problem is another spectre, and here the attitude of Roman Catholic authority seems to the Humanist a grossly mistaken contribution to a pressing danger. Yes, there is plenty of cause to worry.

## What grounds are there for hope?

Humanists see the problems big and large. More than half *The Humanist Outlook* consists in essays about areas of difficulty. In all there is a careful and perceptive analysis of the problem. In all there is a note of hope. This hope is always a commitment, an expression of the Humanist faith. For example, Peter Henderson ends his essay on 'Children with Problems' thus:

'Whether or not there is another, or more than one, life after death, or whether there is personal immortality, the only "faith" that seems to make sense in this uncertain world is the belief that man is still at the early stage of his development and that improving the quality of human life in all its aspects is a task that concerns us all. . . . Irrespective of religious belief, Christian or otherwise, or the lack of it, there is little hope for mankind until men everywhere practise what Confucius taught 500 years before the birth of Jesus – "Do not do to others what you would not like yourself" – and what Jesus himself said in almost identical words, as reported by Luke, "as ye would that men should do to you, do ye also to them likewise." [1]

The equation of Confucius' negative statement and Jesus' positive one is frequently repeated, although I find the logic of this defeating. But let that pass. The crucial question facing us is, 'Will men everywhere practise this?' If they would, all no doubt would be well. At least at the godless level men would be as human as they could be. But the whole case is riddled with this very godlessness. Why *should* all men practise this?

Nietzsche was scathing about those who merely played at atheism. Humanists enjoy his swashbuckling attacks on Christian faith, especially the grovelling self-denial part of it which pleased Nietzsche even less than it pleases them. But they cannot find him a very easy ally. He, more than most Europeans, plumbed the limits of doubt. Atheism for him was no easy dropping of a pilot, or disposing of childhood hangovers. It raised the serious problem, 'If God is dead, what happens to man?' From here begins much of the despairing Existentialism of the last fifty years. Man must create himself. The despairing leap. The curse of meaninglessness. The absurd. If God is dead, man is dead.

Humanists, of course, don't go along with this. Existentialism, says a *Humanist* editorial, is 'pure nonsense, based intellectually upon errors of syntax and emotionally upon exasperation'. But the alternative optimism

[1] *The Humanist Outlook*, p. 110.

seems more and more an act of faith, an *a priori* that man *must* win.

The despised Existentialism provides a more modest hope in the words of Albert Camus, 'Pessimiste quant à la destinée humaine, je suis optimiste quant à l'homme'. Whatever happens to the race – and Camus is not hopeful – the individual can choose and act and show himself greater than the absurdity of the surrounding world.

Man's history to date gives mixed and uncertain evidence. Sometimes there seems a ray of hope, then the selfish dragging of the feet plunges all in dark despair. *Will* men learn to 'practise' even Confucius' negative version? Will they perhaps have to be pressurized into doing it – a conditioning which could once again be the death of free man?

The nettle is grasped by Kingsley Martin in an essay 'Is Humanism Utopian?' contributed to *Objections to Humanism*. Over and over again the difficulties of human obstinacy and folly are faced, but optimism triumphs:

'The reaction against the gospel of Progress is of course powerful today, because science seems to be leading us, not to Utopia, but to greater social misery, if not to the final solution of nuclear warfare.'

But after twenty pages of looking at various areas of life he is hopeful:

'We have good reason to believe in the possibility of far greater happiness if society pays attention to ethical principles that follow from the needs of our common humanity. Humanism is an attitude of mind. Some may even find in it the inspiration of a religion. It enables them to see themselves and their society in perspective, and provides a working theory of life which is consistent with current scientific knowledge. It becomes a duty, not only a sensible line of conduct, to work for a world society and dedicate our lives to the still rational hope of progress. The future depends on ourselves, not on any doctrine. We may believe that men progress, not towards Utopia or perfectibility, but towards a happier and more reasonable society.'[2]

Another approach is that of Professor Eysenck. Writing of Humanism and the future, he draws his optimism from the power of his psychological discipline.

'Humanism must adopt whole-heartedly the scientific method: that means (because nearly all the problems Humanism is concerned with are psychological problems) that it must identify with scientific psychology. . . . So far, alas, Humanism is not showing many signs of following the path; perhaps an internal debate might be in order to discuss this and alternative proposals for harnessing the emotional vigour of humanists in a more positive endeavour than the mere opposition to organized religion.'[3]

But to reduce all to psychology is to reduce again to molecule-talk. The spectre of dehumanization still hovers, and social engineering easily becomes manipulation.

## Hope beyond death?

Beyond the immediate (say the next 500 years) future, does the optimism hold good? It seems to be agreed that the human species is doomed to extinction. Eventually all will return to interstellar cold. Life may emerge in some other galaxy, if evolution does its stuff, but our own particular human experiment will be over. For the individual Humanist there is, of course, no personal survival. 'When I die I shall rot, and that will be the end of

[2] K. Martin in *Objections to Humanism*, pp. 81, 102.
[3] *The Humanist Outlook*, pp. 276f.

me', said Bertrand Russell; and in his often-quoted 'A Free Man's Worship' he speaks of the necessity of a 'foundation of unyielding despair'. Only in view of man's transience and cosmic insignificance can firm action be taken. It may be said that he devoted a long and distinguished life denying what he wrote; his labours for human dignity, rationality, forethought and concern belie this despairing foundation.

H. J. Blackham devotes a chapter to 'The Pointlessness of it all'.[4] The slogan of 'Humanist Week' was 'This life is all there is – make it good to be alive'. Meaning is not to be found by reference to a distant goal after death, but you '*give*' life meaning yourself – it has all the meaning you give it'. This sounds almost like a confidence trick. But if you start with no absolute, then you have to import values or live without them. And if *you* have only temporal standing, your values perish with you, except in so far as they have been taken up by other men; and when Man ceases, his values cease. Yet Mr Blackham views this philosophically:

'This is the true nihilism, to take oblivion as the measure of all things because oblivion may be the destiny [*sic*] of all things. . . . To appeal against the temporal character of our life, to aspire to an eternal, unconditioned existence, is not really to look for salvation, for it is to reject and forfeit life. . . . But can humanists really and justifiably maintain equanimity in the face not only of probable ultimate annihilation but also of actual human suffering and stupidity and brutality on the present scale? Is there any satisfaction at all to be found in the general behaviour of mankind or in the trends and tendencies that can be discerned? There is no answer to such a question, or no general answer, for there is no general behaviour of mankind. Everybody must balance his own account here. In any such

[4] *Objections to Humanism*, pp. 103ff.

reckoning, the ready money of daily cheerfulness and unalloyed pleasures is not too small to count . . . so long as there are better and worse possibilities there is time for action. . . . That is the summons to humanists and the summons of humanism.'[5]

## Christian hope

It is a pity that Humanists so often see the Christian hope as a denial of life here and now. Paul spoke of the 'promise of the life that now is and of that which is to come', and a surprising number of Christians do in fact manage to enjoy both. But the Christian hope needs a lot of elucidation if it is not to be thus misunderstood.

First, the future hope is an important part of the gospel. What else can we make of an expression such as this? 'Our Saviour Christ Jesus, who abolished death and brought life and immortality to light through the gospel.'[6] Language fails the writers to describe the 'glory that shall be revealed'. At best they use negatives – no suffering, no death, no separation – and the imagery of light, fruitfulness and worship. Faith will give place to sight, the partial to fulfilment, our hesitant and failing following of Christ to an unbroken fellowship.

Humanists are unimpressed; the more militant secularists find wise-cracking easy. It *can* be an escape – but so can a good income and a happy family be an escape from social responsibility. The crucial experiment is not open to anyone before death. Platonic argument about immortality is not compelling, nor very Christian either, since Christian belief is not in some 'spirit' that goes on disembodied. Paul longed to be 'clothed upon' with his body from heaven. Our personality will have some fresh vehicle of expression, or, in the language of computers, there will be a 'new set of hardware', a new machine for the programme we have written, to go

[5] *Humanism*, pp. 210, 212.
[6] 2 Timothy 1: 10.

through. To the question 'How?' the answer must be similar to the answer in Paul's day, 'You foolish man! What you sow . . . is not the body which is to be, but a bare kernel, perhaps of wheat or of some other grain. But God gives it a body as he has chosen. . . . '[7] The life to come will bear a relation to the present life similar to the relation between the seed and the plant, and the mechanics will be as mysterious.

Elsewhere survival is spoken of as the continuance of a relationship. When the Sadducees tried to make Jesus look a fool on the 'resurrection' question, he reminded them of their own heritage, 'the God of Abraham and the God of Isaac and the God of Jacob . . . is not God of the dead, but of the living; for all live to him'.[8] The relationship between God and the patriarchs who trusted him remained unchanged at death. To be linked to him is to share a different quality of life.

The only 'experimental' evidence given is the resurrection of Jesus. 'Christ the firstfruits', says Paul. This evidence seems almost deliberately ambivalent. The 'no-miracle' brigade, of course, waste no time on it – such things just don't happen. Occasionally *Humanist* carries an article or review to give some new theory as to how the extraordinary story arose. To Luke, the careful historian, there were 'many proofs' that Christ was 'alive after his sufferings'. The event is *sui generis*. Every historian must admit that his attitude to the evidence is coloured by his attitude to Christ. Like 'Fact and Faith' films in the realm of design and creation, so in this realm of resurrection, evidence compels one and bounces off the other. Morison's *Who Moved the Stone?* (see p. 116) – the book that refused to be written – seems overpowering evidence to the believer, who is surprised it cuts so little ice with the unbeliever. Thousands of believers have faced death with confidence – not always the 'Come,

[7] 1 Corinthians 15: 36–38.
[8] Luke 20: 37, 38.

sister death' attitude, but one of sturdy assurance. On the other hand, Charles Bradlaugh's daughter 'had been driven to take the precaution of procuring signed testimony, from those who had been attending him, that during his illness he was never heard to utter one word either directly or indirectly bearing upon religion'[9] lest it should be rumoured he had recanted.

By contrast the Humanist attitude to death is at best Stoic. There is the satisfaction of a life well and fruitfully lived. Professor Crew accepts 'the idea that death is the end of me as an individual without any undue disquiet. I have lived a long and a very full life. I have passed on a genetic endowment to posterity. . . . A few of the results of my activities as a scientist have become embodied in the very texture of the science I tried to serve – this is the immortality that every scientist hopes for.'[1] Naturally, it is the bookish who write about their attitude to death, and it is likely they will have achieved the most. What hope do they give to the non-bookish, whose lives have been routine and who will be remembered for only a short time by a very few people? What sort of equality of opportunity is this? By contrast the apocalyptic picture is of a multitude that no-one can number from every race, tongue, kindred and people. But apart from the desirability or fittingness, is the question of truth. If Christ is not risen, our faith is vain. But now, continues Paul with the powerful Greek perfect tense, Christ is risen, 'stands risen', an event whose significance continues undimmed by time.

The second part of the charge is that Christian 'hope' has nothing to say to the present. All is dumped in some metaphysical pending-tray to be dealt with in the hereafter. But Christians can claim a deeper optimism. While realizing fully man's capacity to drag his selfish feet, his capacity to foul his own nest, to exploit his riches im-

[9] Quoted in *What they've said about the 19th Century Reformers*, p. 121.
[1] *The Humanist Outlook*, p. 260.

providently, to wreck personal relationships, they yet
have hope. Man is a ruin, a noble ruin, but a redeemable
ruin. They do not need recourse to the mythical evolutionary (or Evolutionary) process of 'purging out the
beast'. The evidence is ambivalent. Purged out temporarily in one place, it arises elsewhere. The new 'tolerance' is often more damaging than the old dogmatism.
Parents who 'don't care' may do more damage than the
domineering Victorian. It is not thus that the beast will be
purged. Rather let us *recognize* the *sinner*. Not a flattering
description, but at least human. Beasts don't sin, nor can
they be redeemed. Recognizing his sinnership is the first
step towards renewal. There is no threshold of status,
wealth, education. 'The same Lord is Lord of all and
bestows his riches on all who call upon him.'[2] This is the
path of release and renewal. James Hemming writes
perceptively of the 'inner world' and the ravages of
guilt. We need, he says, 'to share ourselves and our
failures more frankly with each other, to forgive one
another and – which is more difficult – to forgive ourselves'.[3] It is a pity he cannot go on to see the fulfilment
of this in the prayer 'Forgive us . . . as we forgive'.
Sharing with others is good, but is still only a human
bootlace. We need something stronger and more firmly
fixed to pull ourselves out of our predicament.

Is this 'instant salvation'? Why then are the redeemed
not sinless? Secularists lose no time in pointing out that
the redeemed aren't all that successful, and contain as
much of the 'beast' as most cultured Humanists. To this
the answer lies in the doctrine of sanctification – the
warfare in the soul. Flesh and spirit – not (as William
Barclay is at pains to point out) 'body' and spirit: 'The
flesh stands for the total effect upon man of his own sin
and of the sin of his fathers and of the sin of all men who
have gone before him. The flesh is man as he is apart

[2] Romans 10: 12.
[3] J. Hemming, *Individual Morality*, p. 147.

from Jesus Christ and his Spirit.'[4] This is the struggle that features in Christian writing and experience. For many – far many more than the critics allow – it is the story of a slow but successful struggle, rarely the work of a week, but over a lifetime showing the peaceable fruits of righteousness. And progressively, too, yielding the inner peace and confidence of acceptance which sets all emotional energies free to serve others and not defend oneself. Changed lives have borne more powerful witness than clever words. It is the Christian hope that this can happen, does happen, at every level, from the primitive tribesman of New Guinea to the cultured professor who embarrasses his colleagues by becoming a Christian.

Is the optimism, then, part of a package deal? Is it hope within redemption only? Stick-and-carrot methods again? What about the 'good pagan', the sincere, upright Humanist? Do Christians not take account of him in their hope? Yes, and of many less cultured, less privileged, because the Christian doctrine of man is not only of his redeemability, but of his divine origin. Made in the image of God, he has been unable finally to shed the mould. Except under the greatest suppression, ideas of right and wrong show through – the law written on their hearts. Love, acceptance, and many of the values expressed in us-talk are built in, and crop up over and over again, however twisted and suppressed. This is part of the common giving of God. Christians hope in a living, giving, gracious God, whose giving does not depend upon the belief or disbelief of those who receive. They may misuse it, misunderstand it, think up clever non-theistic origins for all the gifts, reducing them all to molecule-talk. But it is the Christian's hope that God has so made the world that his purposes cannot be indefinitely frustrated. Whatever the imagery of a 'new heaven and a new earth' means, it is the language of

---

[4] W. Barclay, *Flesh and Spirit*, p. 22. The first two chapters are an excellent analysis of the 'war in the soul'.

optimism, not pessimism. And even for the immediate present 'all things work together for good to those who love God', and their mandate is still to 'subdue the earth'. The very processes of secularization may be tools for this task.

If this be true, then to deny man his Christian hope is to cut his humanness by half – or more. For it is hard to see what alternative ground there is for optimism. Eat and drink for tomorrow we die, is practical, logical self-ishness. The despair of atheistic existentialism is logical, too. But whence shall optimism be found?

# 10 Discovering the human being

## Discovery or creation?

Kathleen Nott, in the quotation with which this book started, spoke of 'inventing the human being'. A colourful phrase, and perhaps not to be taken too literally, but it could be horribly true. It could be that man now has enough technical know-how to *decide* what future generations shall be like. Just as the fashion world dictates hair styles, lip-line or bust-line, so some fearful 'they' can dictate what shall be 'human'. They could then sit down beside their biochemical pavement artistry and display a sign 'All our own work'. They might even have carefully allowed emotions of admiration and charity to feature in their product so that suitable coins were thrown into the hat.

Lord Bragg, the Cambridge physicist, wrote that truth (in his particular field of natural science) when it was found was like 'a blinding flash of revelation: it comes as something new, more simply and at the same time more aesthetically satisfying than anything one could have created in one's own mind. This conviction is of something revealed, and not something imagined.'[1] We may have said similar things about a great novel. 'The author never imagined that; he must have observed it, either in his own experience or by deep sympathy with someone else.' Christians have said the same about their experience. God is discovered, not imagined or invented.

[1] Quoted in C. A. Coulson, *Science and Christian Belief*, p. 123.

The discovery may be unpleasant and may be unwelcome, as Francis Thompson feared the 'strong feet that followed, followed after', but there is no doubt of its reality. While maintaining this, Christians have of course to say why their awareness and certainty should be more highly regarded than the Zen Buddhist's *sartori* or mind-blowing with LSD. They have to relate the inner witness to a whole, rational view of the world. 'Believe and know'; but faith goes in search of reasons.

There may also be two levels: we may discover 'the human being', the common humanness that all share; and we may also discover in each particular person 'the human being' underneath the sophistication and trappings of mass-produced belongings and attitudes. So George Fox sought to 'appeal to that of God in every man' – though this gave him no illusions about the particular man he addressed, as when he began a letter 'To the light in thy conscience I speak, thou child of the devil'.

Not everybody is in the search for the human being. Plenty are prepared to live superficially, pouring themselves happily into the moulds the advertisements provide. Playwrights mock us for peopling the world with cardboard figures, failing to discover the real people that surround us. We stereotype the student, the politician, the teenager, the mother-in-law. Christians probably stereotype unbelievers as badly as Humanists stereotype Christians, and then proceed to notice all those occasions that fit the stereotype, and neglect all the others.

Even if you start digging, social conditions make the search hard, and conversely make the becoming hard, for those who seek to become truly human. A recent letter in *The Times* complained that our 'present industrial set-up positively corrodes a person's sense of social cohesion'. A university lecturer writes, 'A striking feature of our "permissive" society is its intolerance of deviations from the accepted pattern of attitude and behaviour, and the social pressures on a student to conform have never been greater.' In past ages rigid family structure limited personal development and many a marriage was socially advantageous and personally disastrous. At many times rigid Christian orthodoxy has strangled spontaneous devotion, original expression or honest investigation. Against all these – and many others – Humanists quite properly mount their artillery. They might pause to ask if they are really equipped for the task. May they not even themselves be strangling personal development by denying that man can reach out and find God? 'You did not enter yourselves, and you hindered those who were entering' – a serious charge which Jesus laid against the religious hierarchy of his day, and one that might still inspire humility in all who mould public opinion.

## The need for realism

Miners take the land as they find it – they may spend a long time finding the best places to dig but they can't alter the strata. A lot of writing about society says how things could be better, but it's a big step back to how things are. Many social reformers have written their Erewhon or Utopia. We could all probably draft plans for a better world than the one we have. I'm not sure, however, that we could do this *and* preserve real freedom for anybody. Remember the Irishman who was asked the way to Dublin and replied, 'If I wanted to go to Dublin, I shouldn't start from here.' But we've got to start from here. There has been a lot of good and bad in the past. We inherit noble ideals and a repertoire of sordid tricks. Like walking on sand, we make progress at one step and lose it on the next. We shall probably leave a much better social security system than our fathers passed on to us. We shall certainly leave more radio-active rubbish in the atmosphere and sea.

Christians may at times wallow in the mess, but in their more balanced and realistic moments they can at least claim to be taking the facts seriously. They believe they also take facts seriously when they speak of man created in God's image, so the search for true humanness is not a waste of time. They may welcome the Humanist assertion of human dignity, the right to life, love and livelihood. They work together in world and local relief organizations; in social research and analysis; in Samaritan centre and Marriage Guidance Council. They strive to help people discover themselves, centres of experience and significance, needing and being needed, capable of loving and being loved. At this grass-roots level, both recognize the mess they have inherited, the twisted and damaged personalities they deal with, the modest improvements they may hope for in the given situation. It is tragic and ironic that, with another hat on, Humanists can so easily write of how happy things would be if only people obeyed Confucius, or even more positively cared for one another. Analysis does not give power. Knowledge may fail to motivate. Even self-knowledge is not self-control. Still, all may rejoice when anyone is rehabilitated as a person: rejoice still more if some social improvement gives larger numbers the possibility of fuller personal development. The crunch comes only when we ask, How human can you get?

## The Christian calling

The Christian ideal is of a truly integrated life – not a religious bit stuck on at weekends to a respectable secular life, but 'a life made up of praise in every part'. Such people may find it difficult to realize just how great a bar Humanists put on development. Consider the New Testament picture of 'every man mature in Christ'.

We are God's sons; we live as his sons in his house. This is no easy option. It is a position of responsibility – also of perplexity, for previous tenants have left a lot of mess, and we may not be all that much better ourselves. But at least we show our full humanity by looking up to

God, not down to an animal ancestry.

We are not alone; he has given us his Spirit. Whatever the psychological molecule-talk account; whatever the social account; whatever our own awareness, there is the God-talk account that 'God is at work in you, both to will and to work for his good pleasure'.[2] And this is available not only to the rich or clever, the important or the influential, but to all who believe. The Corinthian church was predominantly lower class and had many slaves, yet all could take to themselves Paul's words, 'Your body is the temple of the Holy Spirit'. Here is the enhancing of human dignity, not its extinction.

> 'For none can guess its grace,
> Till he become the place
> Wherein the Holy Spirit makes his dwelling.'

If all these concepts are false, they should be scrapped. It is a false ideal of truth which allows them to be kept by weak souls who cannot aspire to live in cold rational autonomy. If they are possible, it is no service to say how little they are realized at present. It would be more sensible to put all effort into improving the realization, to follow Paul in his single-minded determination, forgetting the things behind, reaching forward for the prize of the high calling of God in Christ Jesus. If true, these revolutionize everyday life:

> 'A servant with this clause
> Makes drudgery divine.'

Yet the more specific, obvious expressions of Christian life are not unimportant. Prayer, worship and fellowship are not to be denied or forbidden only because they have been the occasion of selfishness, ostentation and exploitation. The wide literature on prayer testifies that no-one has yet buttoned it all up. The persistence of the practice testifies that no-one has yet shown it should be given up.

[2] Philippians 2: 13.

Those who follow Christ follow him in his path of prayer, and in doing so find their experience deepened, their sympathy renewed, their bitterness softened, their endeavour strengthened. Auto-suggestion, psycho-kinesis, and many other molecule-talk explanations are ready to hand. The possibility remains that the God-talk is true too, and human beings may enjoy the privilege of personal relationship with God developed in prayer. Nor is worship exhausted by the aesthetic. It is true choirs *may* sing the Hallelujah Chorus to the glory of Handel or to their own glory, but the impression made upon Handel himself is not so easily explained. His valet found him in tears, declaring, 'I saw heaven opened'. Those who have worshipped for years have known similar moments of enrichment and reality – as well as many times of dryness, insincerity and defeat. The fellowship of believers – often coldly mocked by the existence of cliques in the church – is another part of experience that refuses to be reduced to mateyness, common interest or mutual need. All these factors may be present, but the God-talk remains: 'we, being many, are one body'. In the slave-camp of Vorkuta, John Noble found Christ in Soviet Russia.[3] In Harlem people came out of the wilderness and found strength.[4] In the less dramatic worlds of business, government and education, Christian Unions give support and focus common attention on problems that face believers in their common callings. Far from being a stunting, limiting influence, Christians have found their faith liberating and challenging. Arthur Calder Marshall describes a scene where he told a very old friend, a film producer, that he had become a Christian. 'If it had happened to him and he'd told me about it, I should have said exactly the same thing. "Poor old boy. The onset of middle age. He's committing intellectual suicide." And yet intellectual suicide is just what it's not. I have done

[3] John Noble, *I found God in Soviet Russia* (Lakeland, 1959).
[4] Bruce Kenrick, *Come out the Wilderness* (Collins, 1962).

more really hard thinking than I've ever done before in my life. . . . What I always feared – that to believe in Christianity would be a crimping, binding, constipating experience – has proved to be absolutely untrue. Just the opposite; an enormous sense of liberation, of intellectual daring. . . . '[5] And Professor Blaiklock, distinguished New Zealand classicist, has written of the 'elasticity of mind' which his faith has brought him throughout a long and active academic life.

If these things are true, they are indeed a major part of becoming human. If they are true but not understood, then Christians face a major task in communication, above all at the level of living communication – living letters, known and read by all.

Some account has been given of the debate about survival. It is hard to see how belief in survival limits or reduces the dignity of man. Rather it might be argued that he alone can fashion a personality that endures, that his choices and their consequences will resist the erosion of time. The Christian account goes further. It is not only the survival of what has been developed, but the fulfilling. Now we know in part, then we shall know even as God knows us. Even now we have the experience of suddenly seeing the whole, grasping the truth. Allegories from Plato's Cave to Lewis's Narnia Chronicles have spoken of this, and hinted at the possibility of even greater understanding, the resolution of dilemmas, the reward of hope, the full flowering of trust and love. But yet, say the objectors, how could you enjoy this in full knowledge of others being damned? This poses the final, terrible twist to the question 'How human can you get?'

## Take all you will

God gives – it is his nature. Men take his gifts and use or squander them. Some gifts can be taken unheeding, un-

[5] William Purcell, *This is my Story* (Hodder and Stoughton, 1963), p. 92.

thankful, unaware. Some gifts demand involvement – the gifts of friendship demand friendliness; the gifts of beauty demand attention and appreciation. Some gifts demand involvement with God: forgiveness must be accepted as well as offered; trust and obedience are necessary to the guidance of the Spirit.

You can take what you will. With each taking, you become more human; at each refusal, you are impoverished. As long as life lasts, fences are set. Complete isolation is difficult. However rampantly selfish you are, there are some restrictions on your capacity to withdraw from those you hate; however arrogant you are, there are some things beyond your clutch. Often the fences God sets round human choice are wider than those men have set round themselves. The biblical view is not of a God who gives only to his buddies; he gives *to all* life and breath and all things. Paul had common cause with the Greek poets: 'In him we live and move and have our being.'[6]

And if our 'being' is in a different frame, when time, space and molecules no longer provide the vehicle for our self-expression, it is still God who gives us this being. Take all you will. If all you will take is self-hood, individuality, freedom of choice, then he does not withdraw them. Hell is chosen, God's last gift to those who will take nothing else. C. S. Lewis's allegory in *The Great Divorce* shows the growing isolation, the determination to hold on to individuality, the last desired gift. In this allegory the bus-load who visit heaven find it little to their liking. It is not a pretty subject. Christians have often retreated into universalism (all will be all right in the end), or annihilation (only the faithful will survive beyond the grave). It is a constant embarrassment to them that Christ above all spoke so definitely about hell. Perhaps it is because they have not understood the value God places upon individuality and choice. The matter is

[6] Acts 17: 28.

sharply put in Dorothy Sayers's version of the Faust story. Faust, having tricked Mephistopheles, is called to account by God and offered the choice: either to die like a dog, extinct, finished, or else to survive, damned, beholding always the glory he had rejected, rejecting it still in eternal arrogance.

'Judge:  . . . incapable alike of hell or heaven
            Wander for evermore between the worlds
            Unblest, undamned, unknowing.
Faustus:      Nor blest nor damned?
            Merciful God, what kind of doom is this?
Judge:    A loss beyond all loss: to live content
            Eternally, and never look on God:
            Never behold the wonder of His face
            Fiery with victory . . .
Faustus: Either to lose God and not know the loss,
            Nor even to remember God exists:
            Or see the glories that I may not share, and
                in the sharp
            Hell of a lost desire burn on unquenchably.'[7]

No Christian pretends to understand the dark mysteries of suffering now or hereafter. Nor can he honestly enjoy it. But he can in all honesty say that he brings good news of release. It is unfashionable to warn people of hell. Great preachers of the past may have overdone it, but at least they grasped the good news that 'whoever believes in him will not perish'. Bradlaugh and many atheists since have taunted Christ with his dying cry, 'My God, my God, why hast thou forsaken me?' This, they say, is the despairing cry of a man whose illusion has been shattered. Too late, he sees at last the emptiness of his hope. The sky is closed. Futility. So they may see it. Yet the cross is the centre of worship; Christ is celebrated not primarily for his teaching or example, or courage:

[7] D. Sayers, *The Devil to Pay* (Gollancz, 1939).

'Worthy art thou . . . , for thou wast slain and by thy blood didst ransom men for God.'[8] The cry of dereliction is not the index of disillusionment, but the index of identification. He was made sin for us; he knew the darkness of isolation. In the garden and on the cross he shared the human predicament to the full. And by his resurrection he gave almighty token that no-one need meet that isolation and darkness. Through his death he delivered 'all those who through fear of death were subject to life-long bondage'.

And yet – take all you will? It seems too terrible to offer, for many stop short, refusing to take the last gracious offers that would turn all the rest into full humanity.

## When God became man

C. S. Lewis called it 'the intolerable compliment'. Why could we not be left as we were – untroubled by this terrible offer? The hopes of a quiet and reasonably successful life, or of steady human progress in the fights against disease, might be acceptable. But to be offered relationship with God! The challenge to think God's thoughts, love and will as he loves and wills! We might grudgingly admit we could do with a little improvement, but this is complete remaking. To many it seems out of the question, or even ridiculous.

But our doubt or ridicule shows how we have undervalued the human equipment. Man was made for this. Not to rub along in a more or less comfortable groove of daily life. Not even to do great things in the technological battle against nature. Not even to experience the satisfaction of 'me' and 'us'. Beyond all these valuable gifts and possibilities, 'We were made for thee, and our heart finds no rest until it finds rest in thee.'

There is simply no need to 'invent the human being'. It is *there* already, waiting to be discovered and used to

[8] Revelation 5: 9.

the full. This is no vision or fantasy, but is earthed in an event that is open to test. After the messages of the prophets, God chose a higher medium of communication. The Word became flesh. It was no *avatar*, no transient appearance. He dwelt among us – 'our God contracted to a span, incomprehensibly made man'. And the human equipment was seen fully used, fully developed – truly a demonstration model. 'Since therefore the children share in flesh and blood, he himself likewise partook of the same nature.'[9]

Two, perhaps three, conclusions can be drawn. First, the ground of hope. Man is not a write-off. Whatever mess he has made; however grievously he has misused his power; however much the glory has been overshadowed by the grief; Emmanuel, God is with us. He has not left us alone. He has come to bring light, life and deliverance.

Secondly, here is the demonstration model. No need to invent, or draw up the blueprint for the ideal human being. Here are the human virtues, courage, integrity, compassion, selfless service and devoted love, not in word only but in deed, not in learned books but in humble actions among the common people. The word 'love' has fresh content both more stern and more tender than most of us find comfortable. Here was demonstration of the greatest human possibility, love to God and love to the neighbour; love which meant the agony of the cross and the victory of the empty tomb so that reconciliation might be sure between man and God.

Thirdly, not really a conclusion, but rather a pertinent comment. He came to his own home, and his own people received him not. But to all who received him, who believed in his name, he gave power to become children of God. The terrible offer again. Who were the most human?

The offer remains. It doesn't go away just because you

[9] Hebrews 2: 14.

deny or neglect it. The possibility of neglect, denial or refusal is part of the human equipment, part of the dread gift of freedom. So is the possibility of 'receiving' and beginning the transforming friendship. The refusal is negative, reducing humanity by its most vital dimension. The 'receiving' is positive, liberating, renewing. 'Let not the wise man glory in his wisdom, let not the mighty man glory in his might, let not the rich man glory in his riches; but let him who glories glory in this, that he understands and knows me, that I am the Lord who practise steadfast love, justice, and righteousness.'[1]

[1] Jeremiah 9: 23, 24.